how2become

A FIREFIGHTER
The Insider's Guide

HODDER
EDUCATION
AN HACHETTE UK COMPANY

Orders: Please contact Bookpoint Ltd, 130 Milton Park, Abingdon, Oxon
OX14 4SB. Telephone: (44) 01235 827720, Fax: (44) 01235 400454.
Lines are open from 9.00 to 5.00, Monday to Saturday, with a 24-hour
message answering service. You can also order through our website
www.hoddereducation.co.uk

British Library Cataloguing in Publication Data
A catalogue record for this title is available from the British Library.

ISBN: 978 1444 107852

First published   2009
Impression number 10 9 8 7 6 5 4 3 2 1
Year   2015 2014 2013 2012 2011 2010 2009

Typeset by Servis Filmsetting Ltd, Stockport, Cheshire.
Printed in Great Britain for Hodder Education, An Hachette UK Company,
338 Euston Road, London NW1 3BH by Cox & Wyman Ltd, Reading,
Berkshire.

Hachette UK's policy is to use papers that are natural, renewable and
recyclable products and made from wood grown in sustainable forests.
The logging and manufacturing processes are expected to conform to the
environmental regulations of the country of origin.

A FIREFIGHTER
The Insider's Guide

CONTENTS

INTRODUCTION

Welcome to *how2become a Firefighter: The Insider's Guide*. This guide has been designed to help you prepare for and pass the firefighter selection process.

The author of this guide, Richard McMunn, spent more than 16 years in the UK Fire Service. He worked at many different fire stations in every position up to Station Manager, and he has also sat on numerous interview panels assessing potential candidates to join the service. You will find his advice invaluable and inspiring in your pursuit of joining what is probably one of the most exciting careers available.

While the selection process to join the Fire Service is highly competitive, there are a number of things you can do in order to improve your chances of success, and they are all contained within this guide.

The guide itself has been divided into useful sections to make it easier for you to prepare for each stage. Read each section carefully and take notes as you progress. Don't ever give up on your dreams; if you really want to become a firefighter then

you *can* do it. The way to prepare for a job in the Fire Service is to embark on a programme of 'in-depth' preparation, and this guide will show you exactly how to do that.

If you need any help with motivation, getting fit or interview technique advice, then we offer a wide range of products to assist you. These are all available through our online shop www.how2become.co.uk. We also run a one-day intensive Become a Firefighter course. Details of the course are available at the website www.FirefighterCourse.co.uk.

Once again, thank you for your custom and we wish you every success in your pursuit of a career as a firefighter.

Work hard, stay focused and be what you want . . .

Best wishes

The how2become team

The how2become Team

PREFACE

by author Richard McMunn

I joined the Fire Service on 25 January 1993 after completing four years in the Fleet Air Arm branch of the Royal Navy. In the build-up to joining the Fire Service I embarked on a comprehensive training programme that would see me pass the selection process with relative ease. The reason why I passed the selection process with ease was solely due to the preparation and hard work that I had put in during the build-up.

I have always been a great believer in preparation. Preparation was my key to success, and it is also yours. Without the right level of preparation you will be setting out on the route to failure. The Fire Service is very hard to join, but if you follow the steps that I have compiled within this guide then you will increase your chances of success dramatically. Remember, you are learning how to be a successful candidate, not a successful firefighter!

The Fire Service has changed a great deal over the past few years and even more so in how it assesses potential candidates for firefighter positions. When I joined in 1993,

it helped if you were 6ft (183 cm) tall, built like a mountain and from a military background. Things have certainly changed since then, and rightly so. Yes, the Fire Service still needs people of that calibre but it also needs people who represent the community in which it serves. It needs people from different backgrounds, different cultures, different ages, different sexual orientations and different genders. Basically, the community in which we live is diverse in nature, and therefore so should be the Fire Service if it is to provide a high level of service the public deserve. Most of us, thankfully, will go through life never having to call upon the Fire Service. Those who do call on the Fire Service expect their firefighters to be physically fit, professional and highly competent in their role.

During my time in the Fire Service I attended hundreds of different incidents ranging from property fires, road traffic collisions, chemical incidents, ship fires and even rail accidents. During every single one of them I gave my all, and so did my colleagues. During your time in the Fire Service you will experience many highs and many lows. The highs will come from your ability and influence to save a person's life, and naturally the lows will come from the people whom, sadly, you could not help. How you handle the low points of your career is crucial. Fortunately, you will experience an amazing level of comradeship during your career that is extremely rare and is not normally found in other jobs or professions. It is this high level of comradeship that will get you through the low points.

The men and women of the UK Fire Service carry out an amazing job. They are there to protect the community in which they serve and they do that job with great pride, passion and very high levels of professionalism and commitment. They are to be congratulated for the service they provide.

Before you apply to join the Fire Service, you need to be fully confident that you too are capable of providing that same level of service. If you think you can do it, and you can rise to

the challenge, then you just might be the type of person the Fire Service is looking for.

As you progress through this guide you will notice that the qualities required to be a firefighter are a common theme. You must learn these qualities, and also be able to demonstrate throughout the selection process that you have them, if you are to have any chance of successfully passing the selection process.

ACKNOWLEDGEMENTS

I would like to thank all of the incredible and amazing people I have worked with during my Fire Service career. Their constant desire to improve and provide an excellent service to the public has always inspired me.

I would also like to acknowledge the Fire Brigades Union for the continued and unwavering work that they do for their members – keep up the good work!

I owe thanks to Alison Frecknall of Hodder Education for making this book happen. Thank you for your belief in my product and for your support.

Over the past few years I have taught many candidates on my 'how2become a Firefighter' course. The motivation and desire of these people is uplifting and many of them have proved that if you work hard, and are prepared to put in the effort, you can become a firefighter. Many of them are now serving firefighters.

Finally, I would like to dedicate this book to my mother Pauline, who has always believed in me and stood by me through thick and thin.

Good luck to all of you who want to become firefighters,

Richard McMunn

CHAPTER I
HOW TO PASS THE FIREFIGHTER SELECTION PROCESS

Before I teach you how to pass the firefighter selection process, I want to explain a little bit about the thought process I have used many times in the past when applying for different careers or promotions. This process is a simple one, but it works extremely well. I urge you to use it.

The first thing I always do is put myself in the shoes of the person who is assessing me at each particular stage of the selection process. So, to begin with, I will think about the person who is marking my application form and I will ask myself the following two questions:

Q1. What would they want to see in a successful application?

Q2. How do they feel about marking all of these application forms?

 how2become

Then, I simply write down my perceived answers to these questions, and I get the following responses:

A1. They want to see a well-written, concise, and easy-to-read application that demonstrates that the applicant has the potential to do the job. They also want to see that the applicant has followed all of the information provided in the guidance notes.

A2. They will most probably become bored with marking all of these application forms, especially if they have been marking them for days on end!

Once I have my two answers I will then set out a very simple plan that dictates exactly what I am going to write. In this particular case it will look something like this:

- I will make sure that I read all of the information contained within the guidance notes before I start to complete the application form. I will also highlight the key areas within the guidance notes that I must follow. If I do not follow the guidance notes carefully then my application may be rejected.

- When writing my application I will make sure that it is easy to read, concise and that it answers the questions exactly as required. It is my job to make the application form easy to mark. If the assessor has been marking scores of applications, then I want to make it easy for them.

I have marked hundreds of application forms in my time and I have also sat on many different interview panels as an assessor. I know exactly what the assessors are looking for in potential firefighters and if you follow this simple format at every stage of the selection process then you will be a far better candidate. At the beginning of each stage of the selection process it is important to set out your plan of how you intend to pass.

The first stage in your preparation is to learn about the role of a firefighter. Before you start to complete the application form you must learn the role and understand exactly what it entails.

CHAPTER 2

THE ROLE OF A FIREFIGHTER

What is a firefighter? This may sound like a silly question with an obvious answer. Of course, the majority of people would say that a firefighter is someone who puts out fires. Yes, they would be correct in that assumption, but the role of a firefighter has changed dramatically over the last 50 years.

What the role entails

Before you apply to become a firefighter it is important that you understand what the role entails. While attending operational incidents is still very much a core part of the role, the majority of your time will be spent working towards educating the public and also preventing incidents from occurring in the first place.

As a professional firefighter you can expect to attend a number of operational incidents, some of which are listed below.

Accidental dwelling fires

This type of fire is exactly as it says – accidental. Somebody in the home may have started a fire by accident. For example, somebody may return from the pub late at night and decide they want to grill some food. Unfortunately, the effects of alcohol or even drugs can send people to sleep and help them to forget the important aspect of safety. Before they know it they are awoken by the sound of a smoke alarm (providing they have one fitted) and a serious fire in the kitchen caused by unattended food left under the grill or even a chip pan.

NEVER pour water onto a burning chip pan. This is one of the key messages that you will be telling the public time and time again.

There are a number of different ways in which accidental dwelling fires can occur:

- faulty electrical goods or wiring that has not been tested or maintained
- overloaded electrical sockets
- cooking left unattended
- chimney fires as a result of the chimney or flue not being cleaned.

Part of the firefighter's role involves educating members of the public about this type of incident and helping them to reduce the chance of a fire occurring in the first place.

Deliberate fires

Deliberate fires are the most common type of fire that you will attend. These can vary in degree and type and are a constant problem for the Fire Service up and down the country. These can range from a small bin fire in a high street or park, which has been set alight deliberately, or even a stolen car that has been set alight to hide any forensic evidence. Examples of deliberate fires are set out below:

Deliberate rubbish fires
This type of fire usually occurs where a quantity of rubbish has been left out by the occupier of a shop, home or business. If you drive around in your car or walk around the street, you will be able to see rubbish carelessly discarded. This is a potential target for the arsonist and you will attend many fires of this nature.

Deliberate car/vehicle fires
Sometimes car thieves and joyriders steal cars for various reasons. You will almost certainly find yourself attending car fires in the middle of the night involving vehicles that have been stolen, abandoned and then set alight. This type of fire can be particularly hazardous owing to the chemicals, foams and other complex materials used in the manufacture of vehicles. During this type of incident you will be required to wear breathing apparatus in order to reduce the risk of smoke inhalation.

Chemical incidents

This type of incident is especially dangerous and hazardous to the firefighter.

As a firefighter you will be occasionally called to incidents that involve the spillage, mishandling, careless disposal or discovery of an unknown or potentlally dangerous substance.

You will flnd that each individual Fire Service has its own operational procedures for this type of incident and you will be fully trained to deal with this type of emergency.

Firefighters always wear operational personal protective equipment, otherwise known as PPE, and this will be discussed later in this guide.

Road Traffic Collisions (RTCs)

Every year, hundreds of people die or are seriously injured in road traffic collisions up and down the country. It is an

unfortunate fact that people still speed, drink and drive, or drive without due care and attention. Although modern safety standards have improved massively over recent years, some people's attitudes to the roads have not.

You will often attend incidents of an unpleasant nature where casualties are often trapped in a vehicle as a result of a collision or accident. This type of work requires amazing levels of professional skill from the firefighter carefully to extract the person trapped inside. You will be equipped with special tools to carry out your task, which are more commonly known as hydraulic rescue equipment.

This type of machinery, operated by hydraulic methods, has the capability of moving great weights in any direction and is designed to help the firefighter create space in which to work, so the casualty can be freed without further injury. Some of the equipment firefighters use while attending this type of incident is extremely versatile and powerful. Hydraulic rescue tools can come in many shapes, forms and sizes. Hydraulic spreading tools can be used to open trapped doors or they can even spread open bars on gates or fences to release a person who is trapped. During incidents of this nature it is important that you remain calm and remember your training. Children often become more distressed than adults in these types of incidents and you must bear this in mind when working to free a casualty.

You will find that you need to work closely with the police and ambulance crews at these incidents and, in particular, listen and take advice from the paramedics when appropriate. They will be able to guide you regarding how long you have to remove the casualty and inform you of any injuries he or she may have sustained. You will be directed and supervised by a supervisory manager at the scene and it will be their job to liaise frequently with the other services.

During your career you may be called upon to free people who have become trapped under buildings or vehicles. Most Fire Services use 'air bags', which can be inflated under

enormous air pressure to remove the obstruction. During your training you will learn a huge amount of job relevant information and procedures which will enable you to carry out your role effectively and competently.

Animal rescues

There will certainly be times when you are called upon to rescue a trapped or injured animal from a variety of situations. You will certainly attend incidents where cows or horses have become stuck in mud or have found their way into ponds, lakes, rivers or canals and they cannot get out. The difficulty in this type of situation is that the animal usually does not want to be rescued and is fearful of the team trying to rescue it.

Once again, specialist teams are trained to deal with these incidents but you may be required to provide a general support role if not directly involved in the rescue.

Personal Protective Equipment (PPE)

As with all jobs where a hazard or risk is involved, you'll be required to wear protective clothing. Within the Fire Service this is more commonly known as Personal Protective Equipment (PPE) and covers a wide range of clothing and equipment from fire tunics, gloves, boots and helmets, to breathing apparatus, safety glasses and impact shields.

When you join the Fire Service and become a firefighter, you will be issued with your own PPE, which includes fire boots, protective tunic and leggings, firefighting gloves, a flash-hood and a helmet. It will be your responsibility to check your equipment at the beginning of each shift to ensure that it provides you with a high level of personal protection.

Fire tunics and leggings

These form the main body of the firefighter's protection and cover the main torso or body area. They are always made of

fabric containing fire-resistant qualities of varying grades and must meet specific standards in relation to protection. Not all fire services have the same style of uniform or colour. For example, some fire services use the colour purple, which is a more unconventional colour of PPE. This colour is highly reflective in a fire and affords great protection. More common colours include blue and gold.

Gloves, boots and helmet

To provide you with full protection, you will be required to wear gloves, boots and a helmet while attending the majority of operational incidents. Once again, these must meet stringent regulations in relation to build quality, design and safety. Each Fire Service will buy a different type and style depending on its individual budgets and requirements.

Flash-hood

This is an extremely important part of the firefighter's uniform and must always be worn while attending incidents. The flash-hood protects the main head portion and neck from heat, fire and flame. It is designed specifically to withstand high temperatures and will provide you with a certain amount of protection when fighting fires both internally and externally. Firefighters wear flash-hoods to protect themselves from flash burns and scalds.

Breathing apparatus

Breathing apparatus (BA) is used by firefighters when entering a building or premises to tackle a fire. It can also be used externally when tackling car fires or barn fires to provide 'comfort' to the wearer and prevent him or her from breathing in the toxic fumes or smoke. Many years ago firefighters 'donned' breathing apparatus only as a last resort, whereas now it is seen as a vital part of the firefighter's PPE.

The breathing apparatus set consists of a harness configuration, which incorporates adjustable straps to give the wearer maximum comfort. It will also contain a cylinder, usually of a lightweight construction, containing compressed air that the user will draw on through the facemask.

During your training to become a firefighter you will attend a specialised course in relation to the procedures for correctly wearing breathing apparatus.

We have now completed our insight into the role of a firefighter. Of course, there are many different aspects to the role including training and familiarisation visits, but this will give you a good start into understanding the role and the types of incidents you will attend. During the application form stage of the selection process, and also during the interview, you will more than likely be asked what you think the role involves. In addition to reading the information that is contained within this guide, you are advised to do the following:

- Visit your local fire station and ask the firefighters what their role involves including a typical day.

- Visit the website of the Fire Service you are applying to join and find out what the firefighter's role involves within that particular county or area.

We will now take a brief look at the role structure of the Fire Service.

The role structure within the Fire Service

As a firefighter, you will need to be aware of the different roles each person plays within the Fire Service. Each position along the chain holds a level of responsibility, which will vary according to the Fire Service that you decide to join. A brief description of each role is outlined below.

Firefighter

Firefighters are responsible for operational firefighting duties and responding to incidents as required. They are also responsible for carrying out Community Fire Safety work as required (see Community Fire Safety later in this chapter). Within some Fire Service organisations firefighters are sometimes given the option to work in specific specialised fields such as Technical Fire Safety (see Technical Fire Safety later in this chapter).

Crew Manager

The crew manager is usually the person in charge of a fire engine but, again, he or she may work in other specialised areas such as training, community fire safety or technical fire safety.

Watch Manager

Watch managers can be either in charge of a watch or a fire engine. They can also work in specialised roles such as Technical Fire Safety or Community Fire Safety and even training.

Station Manager

Station managers can be the person in charge of a watch, a fire station, or even a group of fire stations depending on the Fire Service in question. Technical Fire Safety Inspecting Officers usually hold this role. Once again, the station manager may work in a specialised role away from operational duties.

Group Manager

Group managers are usually responsible for a group of fire stations or a division/area.

Area Manager

Area managers are usually responsible for a division or a large area.

Assistant Chief Fire Officer

The assistant to the Chief Fire Officer may also be responsible for a large area or division.

Chief Fire Officer/Brigade Manager

This is the person who has overall responsibility for the management of the Fire Service. He or she will be responsible to the county council or local authority for the efficient running of the Fire Service.

Over the next few pages we will look at a number of important aspects that relate to the firefighter's role including Networking for Women in the Fire Service, equality and fairness in the Fire Service, a typical shift pattern, Community Fire Safety, Technical Fire Safety and risk assessment. Make sure you read all of the information carefully and take notes as you progress. It Is essential that you have a broad knowledge of the firefighter's role before you apply.

Networking for Women in the Fire Service (NWFS)

More and more women are starting to choose a career within the Fire Service – and about time too! As I mentioned at the beginning of this guide, the community in which we live is diverse in nature, and therefore so should the Fire Service be if it is to provide a high level of service to the community.

There are many different support services for women who work in the Fire Service and one of the more prominent is called Networking for Women in the Fire Service (NFWS).

NWFS was established in 1993 as a self-help group for women who were serving in the Fire Service. Over recent

years, NWFS has sought to influence the equality agenda, engaging with the major players in order to ensure the voice of all women in the Fire and Rescue Service is heard.

NWFS is an independent voluntary group of people who aim to contribute to making the Fire Service a place where women and men can work together harmoniously and professionally, and to contribute to developing a thriving Fire Service that supports and actively encourages women in achieving their full potential within the service.

The aim of NWFS

- Ensuring that the Fire Service consistently demonstrates that it values women.

- Contributing to achieving a gender, ethnicity and sexual orientation balance across the rank and role structure consistent with the proportion of women in the active population.

- Having a voice in influencing policy.

- Having a working environment and equipment of the right quality and standards in order to enable women to undertake their role.

- Developing an understanding of the competing demands in achieving a work/life balance and fulfilling role.

To find out more about Networking for Women in the Fire Service you can visit: www.nwfs.net.

Equality and Fairness in the Fire Service

Equality and Fairness is a very important subject and one that you should be familiar with when you apply to join the Fire Service. During the selection process you will be assessed on this important area, therefore having a basic understanding of what it means to the firefighter's role is crucial. As a firefighter you will be working with people from

all walks of life and you must be capable of treating everyone with dignity and respect.

Under the Race Relations (Amendment) Act, public authorities (including the Fire Service) have a general duty to promote race equality. This means that when carrying out their functions or duties they must have due regard to the need to:

- eliminate unlawful discrimination

- promote equality of opportunity

- promote good relations between persons of different racial groups.

In order to demonstrate how a Fire Service plans to meet its statutory duties, it has an obligation to produce and publish what is called a Race Equality Scheme. The Race Equality Scheme outlines the strategy and action plan to ensure that equality and diversity are mainstreamed through policies, practices, procedures and functions. Central to this strategy are external consultation, monitoring and assessment, training, and ensuring that the public has access to this information. In addition to the Race Equality Scheme, fire services will also produce a number of other important schemes such as a Diversity Equality Scheme and Gender Equality Scheme.

I advise you to be aware of the different equality schemes for the individual Fire Service that you are applying to join. By doing this, you will have learnt a considerable amount about this important topic before you join the Fire Service and also, more importantly, you will hopefully demonstrate a commitment to Equality and Fairness. You should be able to read information about each scheme on the website of the Fire Service you are applying to join.

'Equality is not about treating everybody the same, but recognising we are all individuals, unique in our own way. Equality and Fairness is about recognising, accepting and valuing people's unique individuality according to their needs.

 **how2become**

This often means that individuals may be treated appropriately, yet fairly, based on their needs.'

The shift pattern and salary

Firefighters are required to work a set shift pattern. This ensures that the Fire Service can provide operational cover for incidents 24 hours a day, 365 days a year. As an operational firefighter you can expect to work a routine similar to the following:

2 × day shifts – 0900 hours (9a.m.) until 1800 hours (6p.m.)

followed by

2 × night shifts – 1800 hours until 0900 hours

followed by

4 rest days

During the 4 'rest days' you will be able to recover from the operational demands of your shift in preparation for the following duty period.

During your shift you'll be expected to carry out a number of duties, which include the following:

• Attend operational incidents

• Carry out Community Safety work

• Carry out training in preparation for incidents

• Maintain the readiness of all operational equipment, which includes testing and cleaning

• Conduct familiarisation visits of high-risk premises.

A firefighter's salary usually increases each year. You can find out the exact salary by visiting the website www.fbu.org.uk.

Community Fire Safety

Most people who apply to become a firefighter will only focus their efforts on their fitness preparation and also on learning about the reactive side of the role. During your preparation, and in particular your research into the role of a firefighter, be sure to learn some information about Community Fire Safety. When completing your application form and responding to some of the questions at the interview, you will be able to provide a detailed response about your knowledge of the modern-day firefighter's role.

The reactive side of the firefighter's role is exactly that – reacting and responding to fires and incidents when the need arises. This is still a very important aspect of the role but it is now only a small part of it. The modern-day firefighter should be just as concerned with prevention and saving life through Community Fire Safety (CFS) work.

Community Fire Safety is a tool used by the Fire Service to stop fires from occurring in the first place and to take measures to prevent death or injury from fire. Within this section of the book we will look at some of the more common approaches by fire services in their campaign to reduce fires and fire-related injuries/deaths. Study the information and take notes, as you will find some useful tips and advice that you can use during your interview or even on your application form.

At the end of this section you will find a small project entitled 'Community Fire Safety Plan – My Area'. This can be used to prepare your own CFS plan. You may wish to take it along with you to your interview, so that you can demonstrate to the panel that you understand this important concept and what it means to you. Make sure you learn everything there is to know about Community Fire Safety; it is an important part of the modern-day firefighter's role. This will form an integral part of your working life as a firefighter.

Community Fire Safety is basically work that is carried out by the Fire Service that is specifically designed to:

- reduce operational demand

- raise public awareness on safety issues relevant to fire safety

- prevent injuries and deaths as a result of fire.

It is important that you take a look at the website of the Fire Service you are applying to join. On the website you should be able to find a section that relates to the service's Community Fire Safety work. Take a look at what they are doing and make notes. Focus on the firefighter's role and what he/she does. What type of CFS events do they organise and how proactive are they? Make sure you learn everything you can about the CFS work they undertake so that you can answer any interview questions based on this topic.

Remember, the Fire Service is no longer just a 'reactive' organisation that responds to incidents. It is now more focused on a 'proactive and preventive' approach aimed at making the community safer.

In addition to Community Fire Safety work, each Fire Service will work with other partnership agencies in an attempt to reduce other types of incidents such as road traffic collisions.

Smoke alarms

Many fire services are now fitting smoke alarms in homes free of charge. The number of people who die in the home each year from fire runs into the hundreds. It has been identified that you are far more likely to survive and escape from a fire in the home if you have a working smoke alarm fitted. As a firefighter you will need to be fully aware of the benefits smoke alarms can bring and the important advice that goes with them. Some organisations call this free service the 'Home Safety Check' or 'Home Fire Safety Risk Assessment'. Basically, this service involves a team of firefighters visiting

a person's home, upon request, and fitting a working smoke alarm, if they do not already have one. An evaluation of the risks within the house will be carried out and brought to the attention of the homeowner so that they can take steps to reduce the risk of fire. For example, advice will be provided on escape plans, the location of keys, electrical equipment, smoking, cooking and any other fire safety information that is key to that particular homeowner.

The following information relates to smoke alarms and will provide you with some valuable tips for dealing with the public as a firefighter.

You're twice as likely to die in a fire at home if you haven't got a smoke alarm. Therefore, it is crucial to have an alarm fitted that works. Smoke alarms are the easiest way to alert homeowners to the danger of fire, giving them precious time to escape, especially in the middle of the night while they and their family are asleep. I attended many incidents during my Fire Service career where people were injured, or worse, as a result of a fire in their home. The upsetting thing about the majority of these incidents was that the homeowner did not have a working smoke alarm. In some cases the battery had even been removed from the smoke alarm and used to operate a child's toy.

There is no excuse for not having a smoke alarm. However, some people who do have one are in danger too. The alarm could be in the wrong place; there may not be enough smoke alarms for the size of their home; they may not have checked their alarm recently; or the batteries could be missing. The more smoke alarms a household has, the safer its occupants will be. At a minimum, homes should have one alarm on each floor – probably on the hall and landing ceilings depending on the layout.

How many smoke alarms should people have?
This will very much depend on the size and layout of the house. If a household has only one smoke alarm and two floors, the alarm should be placed where the family can hear

it when they're asleep – on the ceiling at the top of the stairs leading to the bedrooms is an ideal location. If a television set or other large electrical appliance is present in the bedroom, then a smoke alarm should be fitted there too.

Where should the alarm be fitted?

The best place is on the ceiling, near or in the middle of the room or hall. The alarm should be at least 30 cm (1 foot) away from a wall or light.

How should people look after their smoke alarm?

- Once a week the alarm should be tested by pressing the test button until the alarm sounds.

- Once a year the homeowner should change the battery (unless it is a sealed alarm). Twice a year they should open the case and gently vacuum the inside using the soft-brush attachment to remove dust from the sensors. If the alarm doesn't open then they should vacuum through the holes.

- After ten years it is best to get a new alarm, or sooner if the need arises.

Escape plans

As a firefighter you will need to be able to advise people on 'escape plans'. An escape plan is something that every home should have. It is basically a plan that is designed to help people get out of their home safely in the event of a fire. This plan needs to take into account the fact that it may be dark when people are escaping.

- The plan should be discussed by all the family and everybody needs to know what the plan is.

- They will need to choose an escape route in case of fire and make sure that it is free from any obstructions. Once again, everybody should be familiar with this route. It is also advisable to tell people they should have an alternative escape route ready just in case.

- As a firefighter you will need to tell them to think about a refuge point. This is a room, preferably with a window, that they can go to if their escape route is blocked by fire.

- Something that the majority of homeowners fail to consider is the location of their door keys. Everybody in the house needs to know where the keys are kept, especially at night time. Most people lock their doors at night, which is great for security reasons, but it can obviously be a hindrance or cause a time delay when trying to escape in an emergency.

- Everybody in the household should know what to do if there is a fire. It is always a good idea to put this information in a prominent position, for example on a fridge or a similar place.

What to do in case of fire

So what would you tell people to do if there was a fire in their home? As a professional firefighter you will be asked this question on many occasions during your career, so make sure you know the answer:

- Alert everyone.

- Make sure everyone in the home knows about the fire.

- Shout to tell them.

- Get everyone together.

- Don't delay, as you cannot afford to waste any time.

- Don't investigate the fire.

- Don't go looking for valuables – whether it's jewellery, photographs, documents or whatever.

- Don't go looking for pets.

- Get out, stay out and call the Fire Service.

Doors

When escaping from a fire within the home the occupants should always make sure all of the doors are closed behind them. The reason for this is that it will delay the spread of fire to other parts of the building until the Fire Service arrives. Before they open a door they should always check with the back of their hand for heat. If the door is hot then there is a good chance there is a fire behind it. They then need to get everyone out using their agreed escape route and they should try to stay together if possible.

When escaping they should keep as low as possible. The air is usually clearer down below and they will be able to breathe far easier at ground level. The reason why they are able to breathe easier near to the ground is because hot air rises. The combustible products and gases that are emitted from a fire are hot and, therefore, the cleaner and cooler air will be nearer to the floor.

Once they've escaped, they should use a mobile phone, a neighbour's phone or a phone box to call 999. These calls are free of charge.

Dialling 999

When calling 999, ask the operator for the Fire Service. Speak slowly, calmly and clearly and listen to the operator, giving all the facts as requested. Did you know that you can still make a 999 emergency call from your mobile phone even if you have no credit? This is a good tip to tell people.

Kitchen safety

Nearly two-thirds of all domestic fires happen because of cooking. The kitchen is probably the single most dangerous place in a home. The fact is that time and again it's the same problems that cause fires in kitchens across the country. If people knew what those problems were, the chance that they

would have a fire in the kitchen would be greatly reduced. Part of your role as a firefighter is to let people know what the dangers are and how to prevent them.

As an operational firefighter I attended hundreds of incidents of this nature. The main cause was where the homeowner had returned from a night out, usually under the influence of alcohol, and decided to cook something quick and easy – usually a sausage sandwich! While they waited for the food to cook, they would sit down in the armchair and unknowingly fall asleep. If there had been a working smoke alarm fitted then they would have been awoken by the sound of the alarm. If they didn't have a working smoke alarm fitted then the consequences of the fire were usually far more serious.

Cooking safely

In order to reduce the risk of a fire occurring as a result of cooking there are a number of important messages that firefighters will pass on to homeowners. If the homeowner is called away from the cooker, by the phone ringing or by someone at the door, then they should take any pans off the heat. It's the easiest thing in the world to forget about but it can have disastrous consequences if neglected.

Cooking safety tips:

- Never become distracted while cooking.

- Don't cook while under the influence of alcohol or prescription drugs.

- Turn saucepan handles so they don't stick out (and over another heat ring).

- Keep the oven door shut.

- Don't put oven gloves or tea towels down on the cooker after use unless the cooker is cool.

- Always clean the grill pan after using it.

Electrical safety

Electrical safety is another important aspect that forms part of the Community Fire Safety message. Electricity is everywhere in our homes, and it's a very useful part of our lives. Unfortunately, it takes only one old or poorly wired plug to prove just how powerful it is. The wires don't even need to touch for a spark to jump and a fire to start. People often become too complacent with electricity and as a firefighter you will advise them on what to be aware of. Just because there's no flame, this doesn't mean there's no fire risk!

When firefighters are advising the general public and educating them on electrical safety, they will usually start off by asking them the following question:

'At night how many of your appliances are using electricity?'

The majority of people will answer some or all of the following:

- fridge
- freezer
- clock on the cooker
- TV on standby
- video or DVD player
- alarm clock
- telephone answering machine
- mobile phone rechargers.

Firefighters will then go on to ask how many of these items are plugged into live sockets. The usual response is that all of the appliances are plugged into live sockets. It is at this point that the firefighter will highlight the importance of having all electrical equipment tested, if possible, to make sure everything is working correctly and safely.

They will also advise people to turn off as many electrical appliances as possible when they are not in use. This will reduce the chance of fire even more, especially at night.

Smoking safety

As a firefighter, you will attend many incidents where smoking has been the primary cause of the fire. Fires are often caused by a carelessly discarded cigarette, so you must be able to provide people with good advice and warn them of the dangers of smoking.

Some of the facts you should know as a firefighter are:

- Fire caused by smoking can kill you very quickly.

- More people die in fires caused by smoking than by any other cause of fire.

- Tobacco keeps burning. Tobacco is manufactured to stay alight, especially cigarette tobacco. It can quietly smoulder out of sight, starting a slow, deadly fire.

- Night-time is the killer time.

- People often smoke late at night when they're tired or have been drinking.

- They often fall asleep while smoking or they don't notice that a cigarette is still burning.

- People should never smoke while in bed as it's too easy to fall asleep. You fall asleep, the cigarette falls from your fingers, the bedclothes start burning, and you never wake up because the fumes kill you.

- Never smoke if you are drowsy, especially if you're sitting down in a comfortable chair or if you've been drinking or taking prescription drugs. Again, it's too easy to fall asleep.

- FINALLY, MAKE SURE ALL SMOKING MATERIALS ARE SAFELY EXTINGUISHED AND DISCARDED AT ALL TIMES.

While it is not essential, you may wish to take the time to develop your own Community Fire Safety Plan to help the Fire Service reduce the number of fires it attends within your area.

The Fire Service is always looking for new and innovative ways to reduce injuries, deaths and damage to property from fire, and you may have some good ideas to help them. When you are asked questions about Community Fire Safety at the interview, why not take along a couple of sheets of paper of your ideas.

Below, we have provided you with some hints and ideas to get you started. To begin with, make sure you have read the Community Fire Safety section of this guide so that you gain

---

Helpful hints to help you get started with your Community Fire Safety plan

- Local advertising campaigns – Where would you advertise? What age group would you want to target? How would you get the Community Fire Safety message across?

- How can you increase fire safety awareness in the home and encourage householders to fit a working smoke alarm?

- How would you raise fire safety awareness in relation to chip-pan fires?

- Where could you advertise to get your message across?

- Could you put Community Fire Safety posters up in local shops or advertise on beer mats or in the local media?

- How could you advertise home fire safety checks? Could anything be done in local shops or supermarkets, etc?

- How could you work with other agencies and stakeholders such as local housing authorities, social services or the police in order to get the Community Fire Safety message across?

Hopefully the above hints will get you started.

an understanding of what CFS is and what it involves. Then, take a look at the ideas we have provided before thinking of your own and creating your plan.

Technical Fire Safety

This has always been a specialist area of the Fire Service, and it requires a high level of skill and experience to become proficient in this role. During my career in the Fire Service I spent some of my time within this important discipline. The Technical Fire Safety department of a Fire Service will provide support in all aspects of fire safety legislation to business owners within the community. They will also carry out enforcement of fire safety legislation and work with local partners in order to reduce risk. Some fire services will call this discipline by a different name, such as Community Fire Protection.

The main role of the Technical Fire Safety department will include the following:

• Ensuring that fire safety protection has been designed into new or materially altered homes, offices and other buildings. In order to achieve this they will work with other agencies such as Building Control who are responsible for ensuring that relevant Building Regulation standards are met.

• Carrying out periodic inspections of premises through fire safety legislation. The relevant legislation has been designed to set out an employer's responsibilities for providing and maintaining a safe environment.

In addition to the above, the Technical Fire Safety team may also:

• work to reduce the impact of arson on the business community, usually by way of education, inspection and enforcement;

• carry out fire safety re-inspections which are predominantly targeted at higher risk premises such as hotels, chemical plants and industrial premises;

 how2become

- work to promote and increase the number of premises which are fitted with sprinkler systems and smoke detectors;

- make attempts to reduce the number of unwanted automatic fire alarm signals. This can usually be achieved by working with the owner of the premises where the unwanted alarms are occurring. Sometimes it may just be the case that a smoke detector has been fitted in the wrong place, such as next to a kitchen. By changing the smoke detector to a heat detector in this type of situation the number of false alarms may be reduced significantly.

During your career you may have the option to transfer into Technical Fire Safety, which usually means that you would no longer work the shift system as indicated previously. The benefit of working this kind of role would mean you no longer have to work nights and weekends, which is a benefit to those people who have family commitments.

There is usually the option to transfer back into operations at a later stage.

Risk assessment

Under the Regulatory Reform (Fire Safety) Order 2005, businesses are required to carry out a 'risk assessment'. A risk assessment is nothing more than a careful examination of what could cause harm to people in the workplace. The risk assessment then enables businesses to weigh up whether they have taken sufficient precautions or should do more to prevent harm. The aim is to make sure that no one gets hurt or injured.

Carrying out a risk assessment

Step 1 – Identify the fire hazards

Step 2 – Identify people at risk

Step 3 – Evaluate the risks

Step 4 – Record your findings

Step 5 – Review and revise the fire risk assessment

In addition to business owners, firefighters also carry out risk assessments every day of their working life. You will carry out many risk assessments during your career, most of them without even knowing it. For example, when deciding to enter a burning building to rescue a family from fire you will subconsciously carry out a risk assessment in your own mind.

What are the hazards? Who is at risk? Is the risk worth taking? Risk assessment is an important part of Fire Service life. Make sure you understand the five steps of the risk assessment process.

Now that you have taken the time to learn some important aspects about the firefighter's role, we will move on to the selection process and more importantly how to prepare for it. In the next chapter of this guide I will provide you with details that relate to the selection process that is used by the majority of fire services within the UK. It is important that you check the accuracy of this information before using it, as some fire services will adopt a different approach when selecting firefighter candidates.

The first area that I will cover is the Personal Qualities and Attributes that are relevant to the role of a firefighter. You will be assessed against these during the majority of the selection process so you need to know them, but more importantly, you need to be capable of **matching** them. Read them carefully as you progress through the next chapter of the guide.

CHAPTER 3

THE ENTRY REQUIREMENTS FOR JOINING THE FIRE SERVICE

The personal qualities required to become a firefighter

The majority of the firefighter selection process is structured around what are known as the Firefighter Personal Qualities and Attributes (PQAs).

When you make your application to join the Fire Service you should be supplied with a copy of these important qualities. If you are not provided with them you can quite easily obtain a copy of them by searching for them on the internet, as they are freely available within the public domain.

These important qualities form the basis of the role of an operational firefighter and, therefore, it is imperative that you use them as a basis for your preparation. When you complete the firefighter application form you should have a copy of the

PQAs next to you. When you prepare for the interview you should also have a copy of the PQAs next to you.

You will be assessed in relation to the qualities throughout the varying sections of the selection process, from the initial application form through to the interview. Therefore, it is essential that you understand what the PQAs involve.

The Firefighter Personal Qualities essentially cover the following areas:

- Demonstrating a commitment to Diversity and Integrity.
- Being open to change within the Fire Service.
- Demonstrating a level of confidence and resilience.
- Having an ability to work with other people.
- Being an effective communicator.
- Having the ability to solve problems.
- Being aware of situations around you.
- Demonstrating a commitment to excellence.

Because these qualities are so important to your preparation when applying to the Fire Service, we need to take a further look at each of them individually. Read them carefully and ask yourself whether you would be capable of demonstrating the requirements of each quality.

Demonstrating a commitment to Diversity and Integrity

This basically means that you should be able to treat people fairly, both at work and within the community. Having an awareness of your community is very important to the firefighter's role. When you deal with people, both at work and within the community that you are serving, you should always maintain an open approach and accept differences such as social background, age, ethnicity, gender, disability, sexual orientation and physical appearance.

When you join the Fire Service you will be expected to uphold the relevant values, be honest, and also be accountable for your own actions. Finally, if while at work you notice someone behaving in an unacceptable manner, then you should be prepared to challenge that behaviour if it is inconsistent with the values of the Fire Service.

Being open to change within the Fire Service

The Fire Service is a changing organisation. As with any organisation that has a desire to continually improve, change is a must. In order for that change to be implemented successfully, firefighters need to be accepting of it. Before you apply to join the Fire Service, it is important that you understand that there is a need for change, as there is in any organisation. During your career as a firefighter there will be many different changes to working practices that you will need to embrace. As technology and safety procedures/ equipment improves, so will the need for working practices and procedures within the Fire Service.

When you join the service you will undoubtedly attend many incidents but there is also a preventive side to the job. You will need to be willing to participate in Community Fire Safety activities such as educating the public and school children. After all, their safe future is in your hands. Teach them well now and they will hopefully be safe for their entire lives. In essence, it is imperative that you embrace and support change as a firefighter.

Demonstrating a level of confidence and resilience

As you can imagine, as a firefighter you will attend some tough incidents. These incidents will test your physical strength, your emotional stability and your ability to remain calm when all around you is going wrong. When people are leaving burning buildings, you will be running in, using your skills and your equipment to save life and property. Therefore,

with all of this in mind, you must be able to remain in control of your emotions during emergency incidents.

You must be able to remember your training and procedures and concentrate on the task in hand despite the pressure of the incident, and the panicking public around you. What would you do as a firefighter if things didn't go to plan during an incident? Would you lose confidence in your abilities or would you knuckle down, get the job done and then learn from any mistakes afterwards?

Having an ability to work with other people

As you can imagine, firefighters have to work in teams. The size of the team will depend on a number of factors including the nature of the task in hand. However, as a rule of thumb they usually work in teams ranging from two to twenty people. Therefore, having an ability to work effectively as a member of a team is crucial to the role. In order for a team to work effectively and efficiently the members of that team need to have a positive relationship. They don't necessarily have to like each other, but they need to have a good, strong working relationship. As a firefighter you will work with many different teams including members of different services such as police and ambulance crews. As with other members of the emergency services, you will need to have an ability to reassure and calm members of the public.

Working as part of a team also means there is a requirement for each individual to be aware of the wider team goals. For example, you may be asked by your Watch Manager to give a Community Fire Safety talk to a group of school children at short notice. Would you be able to prepare in time and would you have the skills required to deliver the presentation?

Finally, when you are working in the community you will need to present a positive image of the Fire Service. Naturally you

will be proud to work as a firefighter and this must come across in your day-to-day work. The Fire Service has an important and respected image to protect and it will be your job as a firefighter to uphold it.

Being an effective communicator

As a firefighter you will be communicating with a wide variety of people ranging from members of your team through to members of the public at emergency incidents. How you communicate to these different groups is important. For example, if you were giving a Community Fire Safety talk to a group of school children, then you would need to adapt your communication style to suit children instead of, for example, a group of mature students. You must be able to communicate with small groups of people and also large groups.

On occasions you will need to educate the public following incidents where a person has either lost their life or become injured as a result of a fire. Let us assume that there has been a fire in a house where the owner did not have a working smoke alarm. What do you think you would need to do as a firefighter following the incident? The right thing to do would be to visit the residents in the local neighbourhood to offer them fire safety advice, and to check that each household has a working smoke alarm fitted. When talking to these people you would need to be sensitive to the fact that a fire had occurred in their neighbourhood, and as a result they could be feeling frightened or vulnerable.

At emergency incidents you will be required to send important messages over the radio, either to other members of your team or to the central control that deals with all vehicle movements and deployments. It is imperative that, once you have sent a message, you check to see that the other person has received it. Checking and confirming that messages have been received and understood is an integral part of a firefighter's role.

Having the ability to solve problems

Firefighters are generally excellent problem solvers. They have a unique knack of finding ways to solve problems with innovative and practical solutions. They can usually generate more than one solution to a problem and they can carry out their work in a logical and systematic manner despite the pressure of an incident.

As a firefighter you will need to be able to remember your training and procedures while using your skills to resolve problems quickly and competently. You will need to be safe at all times and work in accordance with health and safety procedures in order to minimise the risk to yourself, your work colleagues and the general public.

During the selection process you will be assessed on your ability to work with numbers. The reason for this type of assessment is that you will be required to apply task procedures using addition, subtraction, division and multiplication as an operational firefighter.

Being aware of situations around you

Firefighters must be able to work safely at all times, both at the fire station and also during operational incidents. During your training you will learn the concept of 'risk assessment'. This is a relatively simple process that is designed to protect you and your work colleagues from the hazards that are around you while at work. You will need to keep checking your working environment for the dangers that are present and then take steps to minimise the risks. You will then need to inform the rest of your team about the dangers so that they are safe from harm.

Demonstrating a commitment to excellence

Throughout your career as a firefighter you will need to look for ways to improve the standards of working. Being committed

to delivering an excellent service is all part and parcel of the job. You will need to be comfortable with carrying out everyday routine tasks and understand that they must be done competently in order to maintain high standards.

Your approach to every working task will need to be professional and you will be required to maintain appropriate levels of fitness.

You will operate under specific disciplinary procedures and have an ability to work unsupervised without being constantly checked by your supervisory manager. In essence, you will need to be committed to delivering a highly professional service to the public.

So, as you can see, the personal qualities that you will be required to demonstrate during the firefighter selection process are comprehensive. The PQAs will form the basis of your preparation. When completing the application form and preparing for the interview, make sure you have a copy of the PQAs next to you. As we progress through this guide it will become more apparent as to the reason why. You should be able to obtain a copy of the PQAs from the Fire Service you are applying to join.

Other requirements

In addition to the firefighter PQAs, there will also be a number of other requirements that you will have to meet. These can vary but the more common requirements are that you:

- have a minimum age of 18
- have a good all-round fitness
- pass both written and practical tests
- are able to work in a 'no smoking' environment
- have the ability to meet specific eyesight standards
- pass the Fire Service medical

- are willing to work the shift pattern appropriate to the organisation you are applying to join

- are prepared to be posted anywhere within the Fire Service area you join

- have no unspent criminal convictions.

NOTE: I strongly advise that you confirm the exact entry requirements with the Fire Service you are applying to join, as these can vary.

The application form

The first stage of the whole process to becoming a firefighter, and certainly one of the most important stages, is the application form. If you fail at this hurdle then you'll have to wait for the next recruitment campaign before you can try again, so make sure you prepare yourself thoroughly.

Most people do not think of this, but it is a good idea to photocopy your application form once you receive it so that you can have a practice run before completing the real thing. A lot of people who apply to join the Fire Service fail at this stage because they do not read the instructions and carry out exactly what is required. You will recall at the beginning of this guide I explained the process that I go through when applying for jobs or promotions. Make sure you follow the same process that I have used to great effect during my career.

You need to set aside plenty of time when preparing your responses to the application form questions. Remember to make sure that you have a copy of the firefighter PQAs next to you when completing the form. Read the form at least twice in a quiet room away from any distractions. What is the form asking for? Does it ask you to describe, detail or give examples? These are all keywords and clues that you must focus on when responding to the questions. Does the form ask you to complete it in black or blue pen or even in

capital letters? If it does, then make sure you comply, as even this minor attention to detail can be the difference between a pass and a fail.

Within this guide I have dedicated a complete section to the application form to help you to complete it more effectively.

Firefighter questionnaire – if applicable

Some fire services may also send you a questionnaire that asks specific questions in relation to the role of an operational firefighter. You may/may not be required to send this questionnaire back to the Fire and Rescue Service.

Some of the questions may be based on the following:

- Are you interested in people?
- Are you sensitive when dealing with people?
- Are you committed to maintaining your fitness?
- Do you enjoy making things or working with equipment?
- Can you be relied upon?
- Are you prepared to work outside in cold conditions for protracted periods?
- Can you cope with routine?
- Are you a practical person?
- Can you come up with solutions to problems?
- Are you prepared to educate people in order to improve their safety awareness?

You will find that there are a number of questions based around these types of topics. You should be able to 'tick' or answer 'YES' to all of them as they are based around the 'person specification' for becoming a firefighter and therefore integral to the role. The best advice I can give you is to write

down **examples** to each question asked, and keep a copy of these for the interview stage, if you reach that part.

For example, one of the questions asked may say:

'Is regular exercise a part of your life?'

Your answer to this question should be 'YES'. You may then be able to back up this answer by saying, for example:

I currently attend my local gymnasium four times a week and stick to a routine that involves 20 minutes warm-up on the exercise bike, 15 minutes running on the treadmill, 15 minutes rowing and a variety of light dumbbell work.

I also play and train with a local football/rugby/hockey team, which keeps my level of fitness up. I enjoy training and playing sports in a team environment.

Be aware that you may be asked questions relating to the questionnaire at the interview stage.

The written tests

The firefighter written tests may vary between different fire services but those that form part of the National Firefighter Selection Process include:

- situational awareness and problem solving
- understanding information
- working with numbers.

Some fire services may use different forms of written test including psychometric testing. Please see the 'Written tests' section for more detailed examples and explanations on the type of tests you may encounter.

The physical tests

The firefighter physical tests, which form part of the National Selection Process, are designed to assess whether you have

the physical strength and fitness to carry out the demanding role of a firefighter.

The tests themselves will assess three key areas:

1. Your overall level of fitness

2. Your strength and manual dexterity

3. Your levels of confidence.

The tests have been designed to reflect operational practice, so they may change from time to time, depending on the requirements of the service you are applying to join. Make sure you confirm the type and nature of the tests you are required to take with the Fire Service you are applying to join.

Prior to taking the tests you will probably be required to complete a Medical Screening form. This will provide the Fire Service with details about your current suitability for taking the tests.

The more common type of tests that are used include the following:

• Enclosed space

• Ladder climb

• Casualty evacuation

• Ladder lift and lower simulation

• Equipment assembly

• Equipment carry.

A description of each test is now provided with hints and tips about how to prepare.

Enclosed space

You will normally be required to wear full Personal Protective Equipment (PPE) including a breathing apparatus facemask.

You will then be required to negotiate your way around a crawling gallery. The crawling gallery is usually a cage or other similar type of construction, which has confined tunnels and routes that you must follow. During the test you may be required to perform specific tasks similar to those a firefighter would normally undertake. Full instructions will be provided prior to the commencement of the test.

Top Tips

The important factor here is to remain calm, compose your breathing and concentrate on the task in hand. Some candidates start to panic when they put on the facemask, but if you control your breathing and remember that you are perfectly safe then you will be fine. As you progress along the route keep remembering to check your breathing; this is crucial. Keep calm at all times and do not panic. When preparing for this test you should concentrate on your aerobic fitness and also on light weight work. The fitter you are, the easier you will find the test. Take a look at your free bonus guide 'How to Get Firefighter Fit' for some excellent tips on preparing for the physical tests.

Ladder climb

Again, this test is designed to assess your confidence while working at height. As you can imagine, firefighters are often required to work at heights during their day-to-day work and training. Unless you are used to working at height you may find the ladder climb a nervous experience. I can remember climbing the ladder during my firefighter assessment and feeling my legs trembling! I had not been up a ladder for years and, therefore, I didn't have the confidence that I thought I'd have. However, with a positive attitude I got on with the assessment and passed with ease.

During the ladder climb you will be wearing a safety harness and full PPE, so there is really no need to panic. You will

be required to ascend the ladder to a given point and then carry out what is called a 'leg lock'. Full instructions will be provided.

Top Tips

Again, do not panic. Take deep breaths and concentrate on the task in hand. You do not need a high level of fitness or strength to pass this test; it is all about your levels of confidence. Listen very carefully to the brief and try to watch other candidates who take the test prior to you.

Casualty evacuation

During this test you will be wearing full PPE. You will normally be required to carry a 55 kg dummy casualty around a 30 m course. Throughout the assessment you will be guided by an assessor, for safety reasons, as you will be walking backwards.

Top Tips

Work on your upper and lower body strength. Light weight work in the gym will be sufficient to increase your overall body strength. This is not a difficult test to pass, providing you have the right levels of strength and stamina.

Ladder lift and lower simulation

This test will assess your upper and lower body strength. While wearing full PPE you will be required to raise a bar approximately 75 cm off the ground to a height of approximately 182 cm, and then back down to the 75 cm level in a controlled manner. At lifting point, the weight will be around 5 kg with the maximum load to be added being 15 kg.

Top Tips

Once again, work on your upper and lower body strength. The types of exercises you may wish to carry out in the gym to prepare for this test are:

- bench press
- lateral pull-down
- shoulder press
- leg press.

Equipment assembly

This test has been designed to assess your manual dexterity. In order to pass this test you will need to carry out practical tasks without difficulty while using your hands. Firefighters are practical people and they are generally very good with their hands. The Fire Service is full of practical people including electricians, carpenters, plumbers and bricklayers. You will be required to assemble and then disassemble an item of equipment, usually using colour-coded diagrams.

Top Tips

During the build-up to this test try to carry out practical tasks around the home or at work. If I were taking this assessment myself, I would prepare by using a Meccano or Lego set and following the provided instructions to build a specific model or design.

Equipment carry

This test has been designed to assess your muscular strength, stamina and aerobic fitness. The tasks that you will be required to perform are very similar in nature to those a firefighter would undertake at an incident. You will be

required to carry out a series of tests, which may include the following:

- Drag a hose reel from a fire engine for a set distance and then jog back.

- Safely pick up and carry two coiled hoses for a set distance.

- Safely pick up and carry one coiled hose at chest height for a set distance and then jog back.

- Safely pick up a large suction hose, including a basket and strainer, and carry them for a set distance before jogging back.

- Safely pick up an object weighing approximately 30 kg and carry it for a set distance before jogging back.

Top Tips

Running and light gym work are great ways to prepare for this assessment. A structured running programme, including light weight work, should normally be sufficient for the average person to pass this test.

During the build-up to the selection process you will have a large number of tests and assessments to prepare for. Many candidates will work hard on their fitness levels and stamina while neglecting other areas such as PQA work. If I were going through the firefighter selection process again, I would probably spend only around 20 per cent of my time preparing for the physical tests. The remainder would be used to concentrate on the other areas of assessment.

Shuttle run/bleep test

The shuttle run or bleep test used to be an integral part of the firefighter selection process. However, this test is now rarely used by any of the fire services during selection. It has to be said, however, that this test is a fantastic way to improve your

level of fitness, and it is certainly worth using it during the build-up to the physical tests.

The shuttle run/bleep test is an assessment of an individual's fitness and it is designed to be both maximal and progressive (i.e. it starts easy and progressively gets harder). During the test you are required to run shuttles between a distance of 15 m or 20 m to a click or beep that gets quicker as the time goes on.

Although the firefighter physical tests are not too difficult to pass, you must still prepare fully for them.

Eyesight and medical tests

Applicants who wish to become a firefighter must meet the relevant eyesight standards and medical requirements of the Fire Service they are applying to join. Full details or the required standards that must be met will be provided when you make your application.

CHAPTER 4
THE TOP TEN INSIDER TIPS AND ADVICE

Having spent a lengthy amount of time in the Fire Service, and having already sat on recruitment interview panels, I have noticed a number of common themes that have been applicable to those people who pass firefighter selection. I have called these common themes my top ten insider tips and advice.

The following ten tips are worth their weight in gold and I strongly recommend you read them carefully and follow the action points provided at the end of each one.

1 Preparation

Preparation is the key to your success.

You must be prepared for every stage of the selection process and do everything you can to increase your chances of succeeding.

Find out when the Fire Service you want to join is recruiting next and begin to prepare months in advance. It is a difficult

process and you can increase your chances of success dramatically by following the advice that is contained within this guide. The competition is fierce and there are thousands of applicants every year for the Fire Service. Yes, it is true that only the best get through the process but what the 'best' actually means is not what you might think. Gone are the days when you needed to be tall, strong and from a military background to guarantee a place in the service.

The Fire Service has changed tremendously over the years and continues to do so. Yes, it is important to concentrate on your physical fitness but it is no longer the most important factor. Use your preparation time effectively and concentrate on the areas detailed within this guide to increase your chances of success.

Action points

Your key preparation areas should include the following:

- Learn and understand the qualities required to become a firefighter.

- Prepare to submit an outstanding application form.

- Spend approximately 20 per cent of your preparation time on your physical fitness, manual dexterity, confidence and stamina.

- Prepare for the written tests by trying sample psychometric test questions including your ability to work with numbers.

- Work on your interview technique and prepare answers to the interview questions contained within this guide.

2 Be physically and mentally fit

Make sure that you are both physically and mentally fit.

Don't believe the hype that you need to be into bodybuilding or as fit as an Olympic runner to become a firefighter. Yes, it

is true that you have to meet a certain level of fitness to pass the physical tests, but if you prepare well in advance you can become fit enough with a few easy steps.

During your preparation it may be worth considering changing your diet to be sure that you are eating the correct foods. Make sure you eat foods that will give you energy and also those that contain the right vitamins to ensure you are at your best. If you think you are overweight then the best form of exercise to take in order to lose weight is walking at a brisk pace every day for at least 20 minutes. You'll be amazed at the difference you feel in just a few weeks. Then you can progress on to jogging and light gym work.

In relation to your mental fitness, cut out alcohol and caffeine in the weeks leading up to your assessments and interview. Drink plenty of water and try to eat your five portions of fruit and vegetables every day. Again, you will be amazed at how much energy you gain simply by looking after yourself.

Depending on your current level of fitness, I would advise that you spend approximately 20 per cent of your total preparation time on improving your fitness levels.

Action points

- Embark on a structured fitness programme that is designed to help you pass the physical tests. See your free 'How to Get Firefighter Fit' guide for some useful tips and advice.

- Drink plenty of water in the build-up to the assessments and interview.

- Cut out alcohol and caffeine during your preparation.

- Eat healthily.

3 Learn the firefighter's role

Learn everything there is to know about the firefighter's role.

Get hold of the job description for a firefighter and study the content, making sure you understand what it involves. Also obtain a copy of the personal qualities that are required to become a firefighter and cross-match your skills with each area.

The firefighter's role has changed tremendously over the years. Yes, firefighters still carry out the important role of saving lives and protecting property but the role is very much more community based, with the emphasis on preventing fires from occurring in the first place. I am not saying that you should spend hours and hours reading about the firefighter's role but you need to be aware of what it involves.

An almost guaranteed question at the interview stage will be 'Tell us what you know about the role of a firefighter.' Your answer should reflect that you have gone out of your way to learn about the role and that you understand what it now involves. Many candidates will tell the interview panel that the job is 'all about rescuing people from fires and training in the gym for the next shout'. While these two elements form part of the role, they are not the most important. It is far better to prevent fires and incidents from occurring in the first place and this will form the majority of your work as a firefighter.

Firefighters spend an average of approximately 5 per cent of their working day attending emergency incidents, a small and surprising amount.

Those candidates who successfully pass the firefighter selection process are able to demonstrate an in-depth knowledge and understanding of the role throughout selection. Read the personal qualities and job description carefully and you will start to understand the role more clearly.

Action points

- Obtain a copy of the firefighter job description and also the personal qualities that are required to perform the role competently. Read them both carefully and understand what the job entails.

- Be able to match your own skills and experiences with the personal qualities. This is great preparation for the application form and the interview stages.

4 Learn about Community Fire Safety

Community Fire Safety is a role that a firefighter must undertake within the community he or she serves in. It basically entails doing all he/she can to reduce the number of incidents that the Fire Service responds to. By fitting smoke alarms in people's homes, the Fire Service is able effectively to make a family safer from fire, if one was to occur.

We have already covered the important subject of Community Fire Safety and what it means to the firefighter. Now go and find out from the Fire Service you are applying to join what they do in relation to Community Fire Safety. This can usually be done by visiting their website. You could be asked questions about Community Fire Safety during the interview, so be prepared! Another great way to get ahead of the competition is to devise your own simple Community Fire Safety strategy based around the problems in your particular area. Try to come up with some ideas for reducing fires in your area. Write them down and present them at your interview. The panel will be impressed to see that you have made an effort to learn about Community Fire Safety and that you understand what it means to your community.

Action points

- Read the Community Fire Safety section of this guide and absorb the information.

- Visit the website of the Fire Service you are applying to join and find out what they are doing in relation to this important subject.

- Consider developing your own Community Fire Safety plan based on the issues and problems that are relevant to your area. Present it to the interview panel at the end of your interview.

5 Understand and believe in Equality and Fairness

The policy of Equality and Fairness plays a big part within the Fire Service.

How we treat people at work, regardless of their sex, religious beliefs, age, sexual orientation or background, is extremely important. You must ensure that you understand what Equality and Fairness means, and the principles behind it. More importantly, you need to believe in it.

The Fire Service wants people who are capable of not just following their policies and procedures, but believing in them too. Nobody wants to go to work and be either bullied or treated inappropriately and you must be capable of treating everyone at work, and in society, with respect and dignity.

'Equality is not about treating everybody the same, but recognising we are all individuals, unique in our own way. Equality and Fairness is about recognising, accepting and valuing people's unique individuality according to their needs. This often means that individuals may be treated appropriately, yet fairly, based on their needs.'

We have already covered information relating to Equality and Fairness, and what each Fire Service expects from you with regard to this area.

I also advise that you find out about the equality and fairness policies and equality schemes for the Fire Service you are trying to join. While this is not essential, it will ensure you

understand what is expected of you as a firefighter in the National Fire Service.

Once again, this can usually be done by visiting the Fire Service website.

Action points

- Understand and believe in Equality and Fairness.

- While not essential, try to obtain a copy of the Fire Service's equality policies. Read them to understand what the Fire Service expects from its employees.

6 Ask questions

Knowledge is power and the more you learn the better.

This guide is generic and therefore cannot provide you with specific details about the individual Fire Service you are applying to join. Firefighters are caring people and in the majority of cases they will help you whenever they can. I strongly recommend that you contact your local fire station. Tell the firefighters that you are applying to join their service and ask if you can visit the station to have a look around. Nine times out of ten they will oblige and will allow you to visit for an hour or so. Now you have the opportunity to ask questions about what they do, what training they undertake, the shift system they work, what equipment they use and how much Community Fire Safety work they carry out. When you visit the station take a pen and paper with you so that you can take notes.

Another way to find out information about the firefighter's role is to visit the service's website. Some fire services have very good websites whereas others do not. Whatever the quality of website, it is still important that you visit it. Again, make notes about the information that is provided.

Action points

- Contact your local fire station and ask them if it is all right to visit. Ask them questions about their role and the good work that they carry out including Community Fire Safety work and training.

- Visit the website of the Fire Service you are applying to join and find out about what it is up to. What is it doing in relation to Community Fire Safety work and has it attended any incidents of interest recently?

7 Be patient and obtain feedback

There have been many cases where people have tried to join the Fire Service on more than one occasion, failing each time.

This does not necessarily mean that those people are not suitable to become firefighters, because many people finally succeed after the second, third, fourth or even fifth attempt! The key to being successful is to be patient and to look for ways to improve and develop each time you are unsuccessful. If you are one of the unfortunate people who have failed in the past, look for ways to improve and find out where you went wrong.

If the Fire Service that you have applied to join offers a debrief facility then make sure you use it. If it does not advertise or offer a debrief session then write in and ask for one. During the debrief listen to what you are told. Accept the officers' professional judgement and take it as a learning experience. This will enable you to improve the next time you apply.

In order to increase your chances of success use your preparation time wisely. Once you have submitted your application form, start preparing for the next element of the selection process. Do not wait for the result to come in, begin preparing for the next stage immediately. This will give you more time to prepare.

So, the main point here is to be patient and use your time wisely. Concentrate on where you feel you need to improve and keep learning as you go along.

Action points

- Don't sit around between results. Start preparing for the next stage immediately. The majority of applicants will wait to see if they have been successful in their application before preparing for the next stage. This is probably two to four weeks of lost preparation time.

- If you are unsuccessful at a particular stage of the selection process, ask for a debrief. It is important that you find out why you were unsuccessful. Don't give in and always look for ways to improve!

8 Carry out community work

Although not essential, it would be beneficial if you can demonstrate that you are, or have been involved, in some form of community work.

The Fire Service is very much about working with the local community and if you can demonstrate that you are capable of doing this then this will be an advantage. This may be in the form of local charity work, for example, or helping out with your local Scout group. The options are endless but at the end of the day you will be able to demonstrate on your application form and during the interview that you are willing and capable of working with the local community.

You may be asked during the interview if you have been involved in any community work, so it will be good if you have had that experience.

If you have not had any experience of any such work then it is never too late to begin. Why not carry out a sponsored swim, cycle ride or car wash and donate the money to a local charity? If you play team sports then you could

arrange a charity game and donate the money to good causes.

Remember that the competition for joining the Fire Service is extremely fierce. You need to stand out from the competition and this could be a good way to achieve that. If I was sitting on an interview panel and a candidate had carried out some form of community work then I would be impressed!

Action point

• Consider carrying out some form of community/charity work.

9 Understand Health and Safety

Health and Safety is integral to the firefighter's role.

At work, firefighters are required to work in potentially dangerous environments. On a call-out to an incident or fire this involves working with dangerous buildings and structures. Firefighters therefore need to be fully conversant with Health and Safety regulations and, in particular, the risk assessment process. At the beginning of every shift, firefighters check all of their equipment to make sure it is safe and that it is working correctly.

Find out as much as possible about Health and Safety, and what it actually means to the role of a firefighter. When you visit your local fire station ask the crews what safety checks they carry out on their equipment.

Every day firefighters carry out risk assessments at work, especially when they are attending operational incidents. Because of the nature of an operational incident and the fact that it is a continually changing environment, firefighters have to carry out a dynamic risk assessment (DRA). The DRA determines the risk factors involved with tackling the incident and it helps firefighters to remain safe and in control.

You may be asked a question relating to Health and Safety during the interview. Be prepared and learn all you can.

Action points

• Learn the 'five steps to risk assessment'.

• When you visit a fire station ask the firefighters about risk assessment, and what it means to them.

• Be aware of the difference between 'risk assessment' and 'dynamic risk assessment'.

10 Written test preparation

It astounds me how many candidates put little or no preparation into this area of the selection process. Again, they are either in the gym or working on aerobic fitness as opposed to working on their numerical skills and psychometric testing ability.

The key to preparing for the written tests is 'little and often'.

Start preparing for this stage of the selection process straight away. Even before you have completed the application form, start working through the sample test questions in this guide. Just by practising for 15 minutes a day, you will soon start to see progress in your testing abilities.

Only you will know the areas that you are weak In, and you will need to carry out some form of 'self analysis' to see where you believe you need to improve. Work on your weak areas!

There are a number of ways to prepare for this stage of the selection process. Here are the most effective:

• Practise calculations such as addition, multiplication, division and subtraction using psychometric testing books and online testing facilities.

• Try answering plenty of sample test questions.

- Understand the role of a firefighter. This will help you when answering some of the test questions.

Action points

- Work on the sample test question provided within this guide.

- Consider purchasing more testing booklets. You can obtain these through www.how2become.co.uk.

- Learn about the role of a firefighter, as this will help you to answer some of the test questions.

Now that we have covered the top ten insider tips and advice, let's get to work and concentrate on each individual area of the selection process. We will start with the application form before progressing through to the written tests and the interview. In order to prepare for the physical tests I recommend you read the 'How to Get Firefighter Fit' section of this guide.

HOW TO COMPLETE THE APPLICATION FORM

CHAPTER 5
APPLICATION FORM BASICS

Important

Within this section of the guide I have provided you with guidance to help you complete the firefighter application form. Please note that the information provided within this book is for guidance purposes only. I have provided you with sample responses to some of the questions you may encounter on the application form. These sample responses are for guidance purposes only. It is important to remember that the responses you provide should be based solely on your own individual skills and experiences.

The application form is one of the first stages of the firefighter selection process and it is probably the hardest to get through. You will be applying along with many hundreds of other applicants and, therefore, your application form needs to be outstanding.

Before we move on to how you should consider completing the form, read the following two important notes:

- Firefighters do not generally retire before their determined retirement date. The reason for this is because it is an exceptional job. Fire services rarely advertise firefighter posts, so the competition is very fierce when firefighter vacancies do eventually become available. Therefore, your application needs to be very good.

- Picture the scene – a Fire Service assessor has been marking application forms for the last two weeks. It is late Friday afternoon and they come across your application form. Your application form is hard to read, full of grammar errors and is incomplete in a number of sections. Do you think the form will get through? The answer is no.

It is crucial that your application form is concise, easy to read, neat, and completed in all the relevant sections. Take your time to complete a solid application. If you have the time, spend a week completing the form and answer the assessable questions in draft first before committing pen to paper. If you are completing an online application then complete your responses in draft first using notepad or a similar tool.

You will recall at the beginning of this guide I mentioned how I 'plan' before completing the application form. Let's recap the important elements of that plan:

- I will make sure that I read all of the information contained within the guidance notes before I start to complete the application form. I will also highlight the key areas within the guidance notes that I must follow. If I do not follow the guidance notes carefully then my application may be rejected.

- When writing my application I will make sure that it is easy to read, concise and that it answers the questions exactly as required. It is my job to make the application form easy to mark. If the assessor has been marking scores of applications, then I want to make it easy for them.

When completing your application form keep a copy of the above points next to you so that they act as an important reminder.

Pre-application checklist

You may find that the firefighter application form includes a pre-application checklist. This is quite straightforward to complete and usually involves a tick-box section.

The first checklist involves questions such as:

Are you prepared to:

- work at height?

- work in enclosed spaces?

- work outdoors?

- get wet during your work?

- get hot/cold while working?

- carry heavy equipment?

- work unsociable hours?

- work in situations where you may see blood, seriously injured, or dead people?

- deal sensitively with people in difficult situations?

- work with a diverse range of people (e.g. of different ages, ethnic backgrounds, etc.)?

Those candidates who tick 'NO' to any of the above questions are unlikely to proceed to the next stages of the selection process.

The next part of the form is usually the personal details section. Once again this is straightforward to complete. The only advice that I can provide you with here is to be honest. Any false or misleading information may deem your application void.

Assessment of personal qualities

This section is designed to assess your personal qualities and attributes against that of a firefighter. When responding to the questions in this section you can draw on any of your experiences either from your home life, leisure activities, work (paid or unpaid) or education.

The questions are usually divided into three parts as follows:

- What you did.

- Why you did it.

- What happened as a result of your actions?

On the following pages I provide some useful tips for helping you answer the questions.

Advice on answering the questions that relate to the personal qualities

- Take your time when completing the questions and follow the advice contained within the section. Remember our 'plan'!

- Remember that you are competing against many other candidates, so take your time to get it right.

- Use recent examples when responding to the questions.

- Use 'keywords' in your responses that relate to the PQAs.

- Make sure that you answer EVERY question.

- Do not go over the allocated 'word count'.

- Be specific about one particular scenario.

- Write down your answers in rough first.

- Remember to photocopy the application form before sending it off. You may need to refer to it before attending your interview.

- Make sure your handwriting is neat and legible. Get someone to read it back to you once completed. If they struggle to read any words or sentences then so will the person assessing your form.

- Read the completed application form carefully before sending it off. The competition is fierce and you need to ensure that you stay ahead of the other candidates, most of whom will not be as prepared as you.

In the following chapter I provide a number of sample questions and answers to assist you in responding to the PQA based questions.

CHAPTER 6
SAMPLE APPLICATION FORM QUESTIONS AND RESPONSES

PQA based questions

Sample question I

Describe a situation where you have worked with people who are different from you in relation to age, background or gender.

This question has been designed to assess your ability to work with others regardless of their background, age or gender. The Fire Service is a diverse workforce and, therefore, it requires people who have the ability to work in such an environment.

When answering this question, think of an occasion when you have worked with people who are different from you in terms of age, background or gender.

Remember to be specific in your response, relating it to a particular situation.

Do not be generic in your response. An example of a generic response would be: '*I am comfortable working with people from different backgrounds and have done this on many occasions*'. This type of response is not specific and does not relate to a situation. Make sure you have a copy of the firefighter PQAs next to you when responding to this question and try to include keywords in your response.

Now take a look at the following example response before using a blank sheet of paper to construct your own response based on your experiences.

Question 1 – Sample response

Describe a situation where you have worked with people who are different from you in relation to age, background or gender.
(Maximum of 150 words)

What did you do?
While working in my current role as a sales assistant I was tasked with working with a new member of the team. The lady had just started working with us and was unfamiliar with the role. She was from a different background and appeared to be very nervous. I tried to comfort her and told her that I was there to support her through her first few working days and help her get her feet under the table.

Why?
I fully understood how she must have felt. It was important that I supported her and helped her through her first few days at work. We are there to help each other regardless of age, background or gender.

What happened as a result?
The lady settled into work well and is now very happy in her role. We have been working together for three months

and have built up a close professional and personal relationship.

Sample question 2

Describe a situation where you have worked closely with other people as part of a team.

As a firefighter, having the ability to build working relationships with your colleagues is very important. After all, they are relying on you to be supportive when you attend operational incidents and also during other tasks that you will be required to perform as a team.

This question is designed to see whether you have the ability to fulfil that role.

Remember again to be specific about a particular situation and avoid the pitfall of being too generic.

Try to think of a situation when you have worked as part of a team, maybe to achieve a common goal or task. The following is a sample response to this question. Read it and make notes before using a blank sheet of paper to create your own response.

Question 2 – Sample response

Describe a situation where you have worked closely with other people as part of a team.

What did you do?
I currently play football for a local Sunday team and we were in fear of relegation to a lower league. I offered to help the team out by arranging and co-ordinating an extra training session on a weekday evening so that we could look for ways to improve our skills.

Why?
I felt that the team needed support and encouragement. We all needed to work together to improve our skills. I knew that

unless the team pulled together and began to work closely as a unit we would be relegated.

What happened as a result?
We all met up for the extra training sessions and worked on our skills and fitness while supporting and helping each other. I helped a team-mate to work on his fitness levels by running 3 miles with him every session. At the end of the season we managed to avoid relegation due to the combined team effort.

Sample question 3

Describe a situation where you have taken steps to improve your skills and/or learn new things.

As a firefighter you will constantly be learning new things. Among other things, you will learn new and amended operational procedures, how to operate operational equipment and you will also attend courses to learn new skills. Therefore, the Fire Service wants to know that you already have the potential to improve your skills and learn new things.

When answering this question, think of an example where you have learnt something new. This may be through your working life, at home or in your leisure time. There are probably many experiences that you can draw from so take the time to think of a suitable response.

I have provided the following sample response to help you. Once you have read it, use a blank sheet of paper to create your own.

Question 3 – Sample response

Describe a situation where you have taken steps to improve your skills and/or learn new things.

What did you do?

Approximately three months ago I asked my line manager if I could attend a two-day customer care skills course. I work as a sales assistant for a large leisure retail outlet. The course was quite in depth and, while on it, I learnt new skills including how to provide a better level of service.

Why?
I wanted to improve my skills in customer care. I am always looking for ways to improve my knowledge and learn new things. I also felt that by attending the course I would be improving the level of service that our customers receive.

What was the result?
I successfully passed the course and I received a qualification in customer care skills. I feel more confident in my abilities and feel more qualified to perform my role. As a result of the course I have also improved the level of service to the customer.

Sample question 4

Describe a situation where you have had to remain calm and controlled in a stressful situation.

Obviously, as a firefighter, members of the public depend on you to stay calm, confident and in control during stressful situations. This skill is crucial to the role of an operational firefighter.

When responding to this question, think of an occasion where you have had to stay calm and in control. This does not necessarily have to be in a work situation but it may be during leisure time or at home. Be careful not to answer this question generically. Focus on a particular situation that you encountered recently.

Again, I have provided you with a sample response to this question. Once you have read it, use a blank sheet of paper to construct your own.

 how2become

Question 4 – Sample response

Describe a situation where you have had to remain calm and controlled in a stressful situation.

What did you do?
While driving home from work I came across a road accident. I parked safely and went over to see if I could help. An elderly lady was in one of the cars suffering from shock. I remained calm and dialled 999 asking for the police and ambulance services. Once I had done this I then gave basic first aid to the lady and ensured that the scene was safe.

Why?
When I arrived people were starting to panic so I knew that somebody needed to take control of the situation. By remaining calm and confident I was able to get help for the lady.

What happened as a result?
Within a few minutes the services arrived and the lady was taken to hospital. The police then took some details of my actions and thanked me for my calm approach and for making the scene safe.

Sample question 5

Describe a situation where you have had to work on your own in accordance with guidelines.

Having the ability to work unsupervised, following strict procedural guidance, is an essential element of the firefighter's role.

During operational incidents you will be under the authority of a supervisory manager. However, there will often be times when you have to work on your own unsupervised, and the Fire Service needs people who are capable of carrying out such tasks.

When answering this question, think of an occasion when you have worked on your own following guidelines. Once again, ensure that you are specific about a particular situation and avoid being too generic.

The following is a sample response to this question. Read it and make notes before using a blank sheet of paper to create your own response.

Question 5 – Sample response

Describe a situation where you have had to work on your own in accordance with guidelines.

What did you do?
While working in my current role as a gas engineer I was tasked with fitting a new boiler to a domestic property in a safe and effective manner. I carried out this work unsupervised and was relied upon to follow strict procedural and safety guidelines.

Why?
If I did not follow the procedural guidance that I received during my training then I would be putting lives at risk. I must ensure that I carry out my work responsibly and follow all safety procedures to ensure that my work is carried out in accordance with my company's policies.

What happened as a result?
The boiler was fitted to the required standard in accordance with the relevant British Standard and all safety procedures were followed. The customer was satisfied with my work, and I was happy that I carried out my duties responsibly and in a competent manner.

Sample question 6

Describe a situation where you have had to change the way you do something following a change imposed by someone in authority.

The Fire Service is constantly looking for ways to modernise, develop and improve. In order for it to complete its modernisation agenda, it requires its employees to be adaptable to change. As a firefighter you will be required to embrace change and actively support it.

When answering this question, think of a specific situation, either at work, home or through your leisure activities, where a change has been imposed by someone in authority.

Take a look at the following sample response to this question. Once you have read it and taken notes, use a blank sheet of paper to construct your own individual answer based on your own experiences.

Question 6 – Sample response

Describe a situation where you have had to change the way you do something following a change imposed by someone in authority.

What did you do?
While working in my current job as a recruitment consultant, my manager wanted to restructure the office and change everyone's roles and responsibilities. The company was performing well but I looked upon this as an opportunity to see if we could improve even further. I fully supported my manager and offered to assist him in the process of change.

Why?
Change and continuous improvement is important if an organisation is going to keep on top of its game. I embrace change and look at it as a positive thing.

What happened as a result?
After approximately three months everybody was settled in their new roles. The change had been a success and our end of quarter figures were on the increase. I now also knew a lot more about the organisation than I had previously as a

direct result of trying new and different things in the office. The team now works better together.

Questions based around your reasons and motivations for wanting to become a firefighter

The next part of the application form may involve additional questions. The following three questions are provided as an example of what you could be required to respond to:

- Why would you be good in the role of a firefighter?

- What skills or experience do you have that you believe are relevant to the role of a firefighter?

- What have you done to find out about what firefighters do?

When answering these three questions, think about what the firefighter's role involves. Don't just mention the operational aspect of the role but remember the important sides of Community Fire Safety, reducing fires and risk, and also training. The skills required to become a firefighter are many and varied.

Make sure you visit the website of the Fire Service that you are applying to join. Visit a fire station and ask the local firefighters what they do and what their role involves.

Below are sample responses to these three questions. Remember to base your answers on your own experiences.

Question and sample response I

Why would you be good in the role of a firefighter?

I believe that I have the necessary skills and attributes to become a competent firefighter. I am a caring and confident person who very much enjoys working with other people of all ages and backgrounds.

I understand that the Fire Service is a continually changing environment. I always embrace change and have experienced it on numerous occasions in my current job. I enjoy working in the community and have experience of working in voluntary organisations and diverse workforces. I enjoy learning new skills and I am always professional in my approach to work. Working in the Fire Service is a customer-focused role and I understand that preventing fires is just as important as responding to them.

I am a reliable, physically fit and dedicated person, and believe I would be a valuable asset to the Fire and Rescue Service.

Question and sample response 2

What skills or experience do you have that you believe are relevant to the role of a firefighter?

I have many years' experience of working in a customer-focused environment where a commitment to excellence is essential.

Within my current role I have a track record for providing a consistent and high level of service. I have sound communication skills and have experience of working in a close team environment where everybody relies on each other to get the job done.

In my current role I am required to work under pressured conditions and I often work unsupervised. I am an extremely practical person who takes the time to learn new skills and have demonstrated this through attending and successfully passing the Duke of Edinburgh's Award. I have good problem-solving skills, which have been gained through my work as a shop manager.

I have a qualification in Health and Safety, and I am conversant with current safe working practices including a good understanding of the risk assessment process.

Question and sample response 3

What have you done to find out about what firefighters do?

I have taken the time to visit the Fire Service's website and fully understand that the firefighter's role is varied and complex.

I have read the Fire Authority's Community Plan and understand that Community Fire Safety, Home Fire Safety Checks and ongoing fire reduction strategies are integral to the firefighter's work. I have also read the Integrated Risk Management Plan for the Fire Service and understand that there is a three-year plan to look into ways to improve the service.

I have taken the time to read and study the current Race Equality Scheme and understand how important this is to the Fire Service.

Finally, I recently visited the local fire station and spent an hour with the firefighters discussing their job, the equipment they use, the working day and their training.

THE WRITTEN TESTS

CHAPTER 7
ABOUT THE FIREFIGHTER WRITTEN TESTS

The National Firefighter Selection Process involves a number of different written tests. These tests usually consist of multiple-choice questions, which are designed to assess a candidate's abilities and aptitude for becoming a competent firefighter.

The tests themselves will normally be carried out at a local test centre or Fire Service establishment and will take approximately three hours to complete. You will receive full details about the tests prior to the test day.

The firefighter written tests are split into two different categories as follows:

1. **Ability tests**

   - Working with numbers

   - Understanding information

   - Situational awareness and problem solving

2. The National Firefighter Questionnaire

This questionnaire has been designed to provide information on your style and your behaviour. The Fire Service will use this information, along with the other results of your tests, to determine whether or not you are suitable to become a firefighter.

Before we take a look at a number of different sample test questions, let's go back to our 'plan'. You will recall at the beginning of the book how I set out my plan for every stage of the selection process. If I was preparing for the firefighter written tests today, I would first ask myself the following two questions:

Q1. Why is the Fire Service assessing me in these areas?

Q2. What would they expect to see from successful candidates?

Once again I will write down my perceived answers to these questions, and I get the following responses:

A1. The Fire Service wants to be sure that I am capable of working with numbers in a fast and competent manner because this is what firefighters are required to do as part of their role. They must use calculations effectively, especially when using breathing apparatus and operating the pump on a fire engine.

The Fire Service also wants to be sure that I can understand information that is relevant to the firefighter's role. This will demonstrate to the assessors that I have the potential to pass the firefighter training course and that I also have the ability to complete any future professional development during my career.

Finally, the service wants to be sure that I am aware of situations relevant to the firefighter's role and that I can apply a common-sense approach to those situations.

A2. The Fire Service would expect to see accurate calculations while I am working with numbers and ensure that I can follow appropriate guidance that is provided during the tests. The service would expect to see that I am capable of understanding job relevant information and of answering questions correctly based around that information. It would also want to see me make common-sense, safe decisions when presented with specific scenarios.

Now that I have my two answers I will set out another simple plan that dictates exactly what I am going to write. In this particular case it will look something like this:

• I will embark on a structured development programme that will improve my ability to work with numbers. I will carry out a large number of sample test questions, and I will obtain further testing booklets and resources to allow me to do that. If I need further assistance or development in this area then I will seek the help of a qualified tutor.

• I will make sure that I fully understand the role of a firefighter so that I can respond to the questions based around understanding information. In order to achieve this I will read and learn the PQAs and also learn about job specific roles such as Community Fire Safety.

• By learning and understanding about the firefighter's role, especially in relation to the PQAs, I will be able to respond to situational awareness questions more effectively. I will also ensure that I make myself aware of Health and Safety and the five steps to risk assessment.

Even though the above process is a simple one, it is important that you carry it out as it will focus your mind on the areas that you need to work on and develop. Now let's move on to different testing areas.

How to prepare for the ability tests

Within this guide I have provided you with a number of sample test questions to help you prepare for the ability tests. Use the questions provided as a practice aid only. Remember that these will not be the exact questions that you will be required to answer on the day.

Prior to the tests

- Preparation, preparation, preparation! In the weeks before the test, work hard to improve your skills in the testing areas. In addition to the tests contained within this guide there are numerous other testing resources available at www.how2become.co.uk. Practice answering as many test questions as possible and make sure you learn from your mistakes.

- Get a good night's sleep before the test day and don't drink any alcohol or caffeine.

- On the morning of the test get up early and have a last practise at a small number of sample test questions just to get your brain working.

- Eat a good healthy breakfast such as bran flakes and a chopped-up banana. Don't eat anything too heavy that will make you feel bloated or sluggish – remember: you want to be at your best.

- Check the news for any potential traffic problems and leave early enough to arrive at the test centre with plenty of time to spare. Take a small bottle of water with you to help keep you hydrated.

On the day

- Arrive in good time at the test location. Make sure you know where the test centre is.

- Ensure that you know exactly what you are required to do – do not be afraid to ask questions.

- Follow the instructions you are given exactly.

- During the tests try to eliminate as many wrong answers as possible. For example, with numerical tests, a quick estimate may help you to discard several of the options without working out every alternative.

- Work as quickly and accurately as you can. Both speed and accuracy are important so do not spend too long on any one question.

- Do not waste time on a difficult question. If you are stuck, leave it and move on but make sure you leave a space on the answer sheet!

- Don't worry if you do not finish all the questions in the time allowed, but if you do, go over your answers again to check them.

- Wear smart, formal clothes. Remember that you are trying to create a good impression. You are attempting to join a uniformed and disciplined service so it is advisable that you wear an appropriate outfit. Many people at the test centre will be wearing jeans and trainers. Make sure you stand out for all the right reasons!

- Keep your head down and concentrate on the task in hand. It is your job to do as well as you possibly can during the tests so it is important that you concentrate.

CHAPTER 8

SITUATIONAL AWARENESS AND PROBLEM SOLVING

This test assesses an applicant's ability to ensure the safety of themselves and others, and their ability to use information to solve problems.

The test requires you to read descriptions of situations or scenarios that you are likely to face when working as a firefighter. You will then be presented with four alternative answers and you must choose the answer that most closely describes what you would do in that situation. It is important to understand that firefighters must be capable of working both safely and unsupervised. Answer the questions carefully and think about the scenario before you respond.

The real test has 30 questions and you will have 35 minutes to complete them. It is up to you to read each question very carefully before selecting your answer.

Sample questions

Now take a look at the practice questions on the following pages and use a blank sheet of paper to mark down your answers. You have five minutes in which to answer the 14 questions. The answers are provided at the end of the test section.

Sample question 1

While using an item of operational equipment at a fire, you notice that part of that equipment is not working correctly. What would you do?

- **A.** Carry on using the equipment and pretend that I haven't noticed the defect.
- **B.** Stop using the equipment and inform my supervisory officer of the problem.
- **C.** Try to fix the equipment myself.
- **D.** Put the equipment back on the Fire Engine and leave it there for someone else to deal with.

Sample question 2

You are attending a road traffic collision as a firefighter and a member of the public approaches you to ask you if it's okay for them to have a closer look at what's going on. What would you do?

- **A.** Politely inform them that it is not safe for them to enter the danger area and that they are to remain behind the cordoned area until the danger has passed.
- **B.** Let them into the danger area in order to gain a closer look.
- **C.** Tell them to come back later and I'll see what I can do.

    D.   Inform them that they can go into the danger area but I'll have to go with them to make sure they are okay.

Sample question 3

Firefighters are often required to enter people's homes in order to carry out Home Fire Safety Checks and to offer fire safety advice when requested. While attending someone's home to offer advice, they inform you that they are visually impaired and that they cannot read the Fire Safety leaflet that you have just given to them. What would you do?

    A.   Tell them that I haven't got any more leaflets and there's nothing else I can do to help them.

    B.   Read out and explain the leaflet to them verbally, confirming that they understand what I am telling them.

    C.   Leave them with the leaflet and tell them to get a friend or relative to read it out to them.

    D.   Walk away and ignore them.

Sample question 4

While carrying out a training session at your fire station you notice that you are not familiar with a new item of equipment that has been issued. What would you do?

    A.   Put the item of equipment away as there will be someone else who knows how to use it.

    B.   Read the instruction manual on how to use the item of equipment over a cup of tea.

    C.   Make sure that I don't use the item of equipment again as I am not qualified to use it.

    D.   Take immediate steps to make sure that I become familiar with the item of equipment and that I can use it safely and competently.

Sample question 5

A member of the public approaches you at the fire station and asks for some advice on where to fit a smoke alarm in their home. What would you do?

A. Draw their attention to the instruction manual/leaflet that came with the smoke alarm when they purchased it.

B. Tell them that it is not my responsibility to tell people where to put their smoke alarms in their home. I am an operational firefighter and my duty is to rescue people from fires.

C. Provide them with a Fire Safety leaflet that explains exactly where to put smoke alarms within the home. Then go through the leaflet with them in detail making sure they understand where the alarm needs to be placed. Finally, provide them with a contact telephone number on which they can call me if they need any further advice.

D. Tell them that providing they are safe in their home and they do not smoke in bed then they should be okay and therefore there's no need for a smoke alarm.

Sample question 6

You are attending a fire in a large factory. While fighting the fire on the second floor of the factory you notice that there is a lot of water building up in the centre of the floor area. What would you do?

A. Carry on fighting the fire and hope that the problem stops. I want to save the building!

B. Keep fighting the fire. Factory floors are designed to take the weight of the water.

C. Tell my manager about the situation so that he/she can assess the situation.

D. Ceilings are designed not to collapse so I should be safe.

Sample question 7

You are attending an incident at 4a.m. where a man has locked himself out of his house. He is very agitated and wants to get in quickly as he needs to get some sleep for work in the morning. What would you do?

A. Break down the door as quickly as possible to let him in.

B. Tell him to call for a locksmith; it is not my problem.

C. Wait for the police to arrive before we break in, after all he could be a burglar.

D. Just leave him locked out.

Sample question 8

You are at the fire station when your manager asks you to order some community fire safety leaflets as she is busy. You go to order the leaflets and one of the more experienced firefighters tells you not to bother as there are plenty in the storeroom. What do you do?

A. Order the leaflets as I have been told to do so.

B. Tell the firefighter to leave me alone, I have a job to do!

C. Take his advice. After all he's been in the job for years so he must be right.

D. Check in the storeroom first to see if there are sufficient leaflets. If there were not, then I'd order them. If there were sufficient leaflets, then I would inform my manager.

Sample question 9

As a serving operational firefighter you are called to a road traffic collision. When you arrive the driver of the car is sitting at the side of the road looking shocked and the passenger is still badly trapped in the car. The police are already at the scene. What do you do?

- **A.** Leave the driver and start working with my team to free the passenger.
- **B.** Leave my colleagues and look after the driver.
- **C.** Put the driver in the back of the fire engine and start helping my colleagues to free the passenger.
- **D.** Ask the police to attend to the driver while I assist my colleagues in freeing the passenger.

Sample question 10

It is 4a.m. and you are attending a fire in a house. You can see flames on the ground floor and smoke on the second floor. A neighbour comes up to you and tells you that he thinks there are two children in one of the upstairs bedrooms. It is your responsibility to decide what to do. What do you do?

- **A.** Tell two firefighters to go upstairs as quickly as possible with a hose to search for the children while two other firefighters tackle the fire downstairs.
- **B.** Tell the neighbour to keep back. If there are any children in the house then you will find them.
- **C.** Get two firefighters to tackle the fire. Once the fire is extinguished I would get two firefighters to search for the missing children.
- **D.** Get one firefighter to go upstairs to search for the children and one firefighter to tackle the fire from downstairs.

Sample question II

As a firefighter you may be required to monitor the pressure that is being delivered to the hoses to ensure that there is sufficient water available to extinguish a fire. This is achieved by looking at the gauges on a pump. At a fire, how often would you look at the gauges if this were your task?

A. I would look approximately every five minutes when I get a chance.

B. I would look when I was told to do so by my manager.

C. I monitor the gauges continuously.

D. I would look at the gauges when I felt that we were running out of water.

Sample question I2

You are attending an incident where a man is struggling to stay afloat after falling into a deep, fast-flowing river. As a firefighter you must not enter water without a buoyancy aid and at this incident you do not have any. What would you do?

A. I would take off my clothes to prevent myself from sinking and wade in after the man. I am strong swimmer and would be able to rescue him.

B. I would throw him a rope and tell him to grab it. Then I would try to pull him to the side with my colleagues.

C. I would take off my clothes and go into the water up to waist height only. This way I would be able to rescue him without endangering myself.

D. I would do nothing. If I don't have a buoyancy aid then I am unable to help him.

Sample question 13

You are attending a fire late at night and there is a large crowd gathering outside. As your colleagues are taking one of the casualties out of the building the crowd suddenly becomes very aggressive and starts shouting abuse at the casualty. What would you do?

A. I would say nothing.

B. I would ask my manager what he/she thought I should do.

C. I would talk assertively to the crowd and inform them that they are causing a disturbance. I would then ask for police assistance.

D. I would confront them and ask them what their problem is.

Sample question 14

A team meeting has been held at your fire station but you were unable to attend due to sickness. The next day you are back at work and you ask a colleague what happened at the meeting. She informs you that you missed nothing and that the meeting was very boring. What would you do?

A. I would take her word for it. Most meetings are quite boring.

B. I would ask my manager what happened at the meeting.

C. I would persist and ask her to tell me what went on at the meeting.

D. Wait to be told by someone else what happened at the meeting.

how2become

Answers to situational awareness questions

Sample question 1 – B
In situations such as these it is important to stop using the equipment and inform a supervisory manager of the problem so that it can be taken out of service and repaired by a qualified person.

Sample question 2 – A
As a firefighter you have a duty of care to protect the public from danger. The cordoned off area is there to prevent the public and other unauthorised personnel from entering the danger area. You must politely inform them that they are not permitted to enter the danger area.

Sample question 3 – B
In this situation you must ensure that the message is communicated to the member of the public and also check to see that they understand. Remember that one of the qualities required to become a firefighter is effective communication and part of this involves checking to see that a message is understood.

Sample question 4 – D
As a firefighter you must always ensure that you can competently use all of your equipment. Imagine getting a call to a road traffic collision at 3a.m. and finding you have forgotten how to use an item of hydraulic rescue equipment. The public rely on you to be able to perform competently in all manner of situations and incidents. You must, therefore, take immediate steps to make sure that you are familiar with the item of equipment and that you can use it safely and competently.

Sample question 5 – C
In this situation you must ensure that they leave the fire station fully armed with the correct information. You must also ensure that they fully understand the instructions and advice that you have provided them with.

Sample question 6 – C
In this type of situation you must take action immediately. The only option here is to inform your supervisory manager of the situation. They will then carry out a risk assessment and take the appropriate action.

Sample question 7 – C
Common sense should tell you here that the man could possibly be a burglar. During incidents of this nature you would request the attendance of the police so that they can verify his credentials and that he is in fact the homeowner.

Sample question 8 – D
The correct answer in this situation would be to check to see if there were, in fact, sufficient leaflets first. While answer 'A' is not incorrect, the common-sense solution would tell you to check first prior to ordering. If there were sufficient leaflets then you would need to inform your supervisory manager.

Sample question 9 – D
This is a difficult situation to be in, but one that you will be faced with as a firefighter. You do not have the option of leaving the person unattended so you must ask a police officer to look after the driver before you go to assist your colleagues.

Sample question 10 – A
In this type of situation you must act on the information provided. However, at all times safety comes first. In this situation you would commit two crews, one team to tackle the fire and the other team to search for the missing children. You would not split the team up, as this would be unsafe practice.

Sample question 11 – C
In this scenario you must ensure that you monitor the gauges continuously. Pressure can change at a moment's notice so you must be on your guard and be able to act accordingly.

Sample question 12 – B
This is a very difficult situation to be in, and one that firefighters are faced with on occasions. You must ensure the safety of yourself and the safety of your work colleagues so the correct option here is B.

Sample question 13 – C
It is important not to inflame situations of this nature and you would need to ask the police to attend in order to deal with it. At no time should you become confrontational, physical, or aggressive.

Sample question 14 – B
In this type of situation you would need to ensure that you obtained the right information about the meeting. Because, in this situation, your work colleague is unlikely to provide you with the right information, you would be advised to ask your manager. He or she would then be able to give you the correct details about the meeting.

Tips for Passing the Situational Awareness and Problem Solving Tests

- Read the question quickly but carefully. Remember that you are being assessed in the areas of 'situational awareness' and 'problem solving'.

- Answer the question based only on the information that is provided. Do not 'assume' but rather base your answers on the facts provided.

- Remember that firefighters must work safely. Think about your responses carefully. If one of the choices sounds dangerous then the likelihood is that it is the wrong answer.

- Learn the personal qualities and attributes (PQAs) of a firefighter before you take the tests. This will give you a good understanding of what the firefighter's role entails.

CHAPTER 9
WORKING WITH NUMBERS

This multiple-choice test assesses your ability to understand and work with numerical information of a type that a firefighter is likely to experience while carrying out his or her role.

The test requires candidates to perform combinations of addition, subtraction, multiplication and division as well as estimations of numerical data. The test usually consists of 32 questions, which must be answered within a set time limit. The questions are usually based around different Fire Service related scenarios, each with five or six related questions.

The scenarios used may cover the following areas:

• Reading gauges at a factory fire

• Monitoring fuel supplies

• Using breathing apparatus

• Managing hoses

- Injuries and fire deaths in the home
- Using hoses at a fire.

Take a look at the following sample 'using breathing apparatus' question.

Using breathing apparatus – sample questions

Firefighters, while attending operational incidents, are sometimes required to wear a breathing apparatus cylinder to help them breathe. It is very important that firefighters can calculate how much air is left in their cylinder. In order to work out how much air is left in a cylinder we need the following three pieces of information:

1. The time that the firefighter entered the fire.
2. How much air in minutes was in the cylinder when the firefighter entered the fire.
3. What the time is now.

Once you have these three pieces of information you will be able to work out how much air is left in the cylinder.

Take a look at the following question:

Sample question

The firefighter entered the fire at 11.06a.m. and he had 47 minutes of air in his cylinder. The time is now 11.17a.m. How much air does he have left?

- **A.** 32 minutes
- **B.** 33 minutes
- **C.** 34 minutes
- **D.** 35 minutes
- **E.** 36 minutes

The correct answer is E – 36 minutes.

11 minutes have now passed since the firefighter entered the building (11.06a.m. – 11.17a.m.). To calculate how much air is left in the cylinder you need to subtract 11 minutes from the total amount of air that was in the cylinder when he entered the fire (47). Therefore, 47 minus 11 equals 36 minutes.

Now try the sample exercise on the following pages.

You have 5 minutes to answer the 10 questions. Use a blank sheet of paper to write down your answers. Calculators are not permitted. The correct answers are supplied at the end of the test.

Question 1

The firefighter entered the fire at 03.01a.m. and he had 47 minutes of air in his cylinder. The time is now 03.30a.m. How much air does he have left?

- **A.** 29 minutes
- **B.** 18 minutes
- **C.** 30 minutes
- **D.** 19 minutes

Question 2

The firefighter entered the fire at 5.51p.m. and he had 44 minutes of air in his cylinder. The time is now 6.30p.m. How much air does he have left?

- **A.** 39 minutes
- **B.** 4 minutes
- **C.** 5 minutes
- **D.** 38 minutes

Question 3

The firefighter entered the fire at 10.00a.m. and he had 43 minutes of air in his cylinder. The time is now 10.09a.m. How much air does he have left?

A. 34 minutes

B. 9 minutes

C. 32 minutes

D. 33 minutes

Question 4

The time is now 03.04a.m. and the firefighter had 44 minutes of air in her cylinder when she entered the fire at 02.50a.m. How much air does she have left?

A. 30 minutes

B. 3 minutes

C. 15 minutes

D. 40 minutes

Question 5

The firefighter had 39 minutes of air in her cylinder when she entered the fire at 11.56p.m. The time is now 11.59p.m. How much air does she have left?

A. 38 minutes

B. 6 minutes

C. 30 minutes

D. 36 minutes

Question 6

The time is now 2.06a.m. and the firefighter had 34 minutes of air in his cylinder when he entered the fire at 01.47a.m. How much air does he have left?

A. 15 minutes

B. 5 minutes

C. 14 minutes

D. 40 minutes

Question 7

The firefighter had 40 minutes of air in her cylinder when she entered the fire at 3.52p.m. The time is now 4.31p.m. How much air does she have left?

A. 39 minutes

B. 1 minute

C. 40 minutes

D. 2 minutes

Question 8

The time is now 8.06a.m. and the firefighter had 47 minutes of air in his cylinder when he entered the fire at 07.45a.m. How much air does he have left?

A. 10 minutes

B. 22 minutes

C. 20 minutes

D. 26 minutes

Question 9

The firefighter had 42 minutes of air in his cylinder when he entered the fire at 10.00p.m. The time is now 10.11p.m. How much air does he have left?

A. 32 minutes

B. 33 minutes

C. 31 minutes

D. 30 minutes

Question 10

The time is now 4.06p.m. and the firefighter had 44 minutes of air in his cylinder when he entered the fire at 4.02p.m. How much air does he have left?

A. 4 minutes

B. 2 minutes

C. 40 minutes

D. 44 minutes

Using breathing apparatus – answers to questions

Question 1
B – 18 minutes

Question 2
C – 5 minutes

Question 3
A – 34 minutes

Question 4
A – 30 minutes

Question 5
D – 36 minutes

Question 6
A – 15 minutes

Question 7
B – 1 minute

Question 8
D – 26 minutes

Question 9
C – 31 minutes

Question 10
C – 40 minutes

Tips for Passing This Test

- You need to work on your numerical skills before you sit this test. After all, you are working with numbers. The tests in this guide are a great starting point. Any type of numerical reasoning test will be a good practice aid and there are plenty available at www.how2become.co.uk.

- You will need to work quickly through each question and, once again, speed will only come with practice! Set aside 20 minutes each night in the two weeks before your test date and use this time to work on your numerical skills.

Further sample test questions

Now that you have had chance to practise some breathing apparatus test questions, take a look at the following sample questions that relate to 'injuries and fire deaths in the home' (fictitious).

Sample question I

The graph below details information about the number of fire deaths in the home during a 12-month period in homes with smoke detection, and in homes without smoke detection.

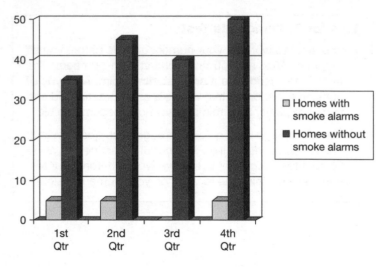

How many people died in homes without smoke alarms during the 12-month period?

Answer [   ]

Sample question 2

The following graph details information about how many people died from house fires during a 12-month period.

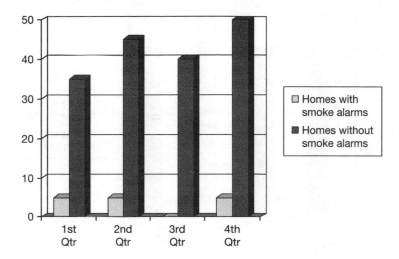

How many people in total died in house fires during the 12-month period?

Answer [   ]

Sample question 3

The following graph details information about how many people died from house fires during a 12-month period.

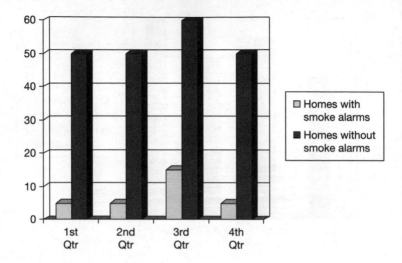

On average, how many people died each month during the 12-month period?

Answer [   ]

Sample question 4

You have been asked by your Watch Manager at the fire station to clean the following rooms: the basement, the kitchen and the training suite. A floor plan of the total area you are required to clean is detailed below (not to scale).

Basement – 60 square metres

Kitchen – 53 square metres

Training suite – 68 square metres

What is the total floor area you are required to clean?

Answer [   ]

Sample question 5

You have been asked by your Watch Manager at the fire station to clean the following rooms: the basement, the kitchen and the training suite. A floor plan of the total area you are required to clean is detailed below (not to scale).

Basement – 60 square metres

Kitchen – 53 square metres

Training suite – 68 square metres

If you were to clean 1 square metre every 30 seconds, how long would it take you to clean the training suite?

Answer

Sample question 6

You have been asked by your Watch Manager at the fire station to clean the appliance bay floor. A floor plan of the total area you are required to clean is detailed below (not to scale).

Appliance bay – 280 square metres

If one bucket of cleaning fluid will clean 20 square metres of floor, how many buckets will you need to clean half of the appliance bay floor area?

Answer

Sample question 7

You have been asked by your Watch Manager at the fire station to clean the appliance bay floor and the kitchen floor. A floor plan of the total area you are required to clean is detailed below (not to scale).

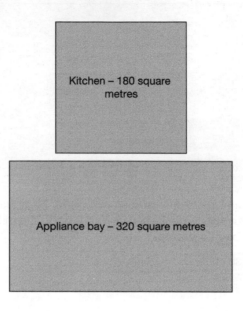

Kitchen – 180 square metres

Appliance bay – 320 square metres

If one bucket of cleaning fluid will clean 20 square metres of floor, how many buckets will you need to clean a quarter of the appliance bay floor and all of the kitchen floor area?

Answer [   ]

Sample question 8

Firefighters attend many different types of fire including rubbish fires, car fires and grass fires. The graph below provides details of these types of fires within the area covered by one particular station over a four-week period. Use the graph to answer the question below.

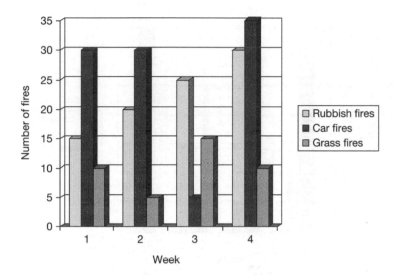

What was the combined number of rubbish fires and car fires in weeks 3 and 4?

Answer

Sample question 9

Firefighters attend many different types of fire including rubbish fires, car fires and grass fires. The graph below provides details of these types of fires within the area covered by one particular station over a four-week period. Use the graph to answer the question below.

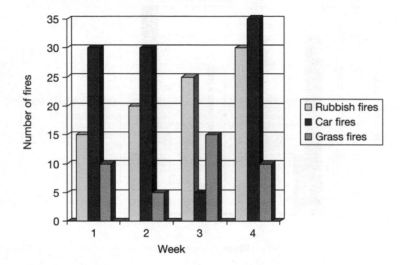

Firefighters often carry out intensive Fire Safety campaigns in order to reduce the number of calls they attend. If firefighters had been carrying out this type of campaign during the four-week period above, for which category of fires and in which week did the campaign have the most positive effect?

Answer [   ]

Sample question 10

Firefighters attend many different types of fire including rubbish fires, car fires and grass fires. The graph below provides details of these types of fires within the area covered by one particular station over a four-week period. Use the graph to answer the question below.

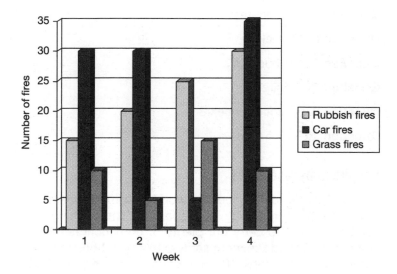

What was the average number of fires attended by the station each week?

Answer [   ]

Answers to further sample test questions

Question 1 – 170

Question 2 – 185

Question 3 – 20

Question 4 – 181 square metres

Question 5 – 34 minutes

Question 6 – 7 buckets

Question 7 – 13 buckets

Question 8 – 95 fires

Question 9 – Car fires; week 3

Question 10 – 57.5 fires

Sample numerical tests

I hope that you didn't find the working with numbers test too difficult. A great way to prepare for the working with numbers test is to carry out plenty of numerical reasoning tests. If you would like more sample test questions then you need to obtain a copy of a numerical reasoning test book from www.how2become.co.uk. Remember, practice makes perfect.

On the following pages I have provided a number of useful numerical practice questions to help you prepare for your tests. Please note that these exercises are for practice purposes only and are not a reflection of the tests you will encounter during the firefighter selection process.

Allow yourself 15 minutes to complete the 30 questions and do not use a calculator. You are permitted to use a blank sheet of paper to carry out your calculations if required.

Good luck!

Sample practice numerical test questions

1. 37 + ? = 95

   A. 85   **B.** 45   **C.** 58   **D.** 57   **E.** 122

   Answer

2. 86 − ? = 32

   A. 54   **B.** 45   **C.** 108   **D.** 118   **E.** 68

   Answer

3. ? + 104 = 210

   A. 601   **B.** 314   **C.** 61   **D.**106   **E.**110

   Answer

4. 109 x ? = 218

   A. 1   **B.** 109   **C.** 12   **D.** 10   **E.** 2

   Answer

5. 6 + 9 + 15 = 15 × ?

   A. 15   **B.** 2   **C.** 3   **D.** 4   **E.** 5

   Answer

6. (34 + 13) − 4 = ? + 3

   A. 7   **B.** 47   **C.** 51   **D.** 40   **E.** 37

   Answer

7. 35 ÷ ? = 10 + 7.5

   A. 2   **B.** 10   **C.** 4   **D.** 1   **E.** 17

   Answer

how2become

8. 7 × ? = 28 × 3

   A. 2   **B.** 3   **C.** 21   **D.** 15   **E.** 12

   Answer [ ]

9. 100 ÷ 4 = 67 − ?

   A. 42   **B.** 24   **C.** 57   **D.** 333   **E.** 2

   Answer [ ]

10. 32 × 9 = 864 ÷ ?

   A. 288   **B.** 3   **C.** 882   **D.** 4   **E.** None of these

   Answer [ ]

11. Following the pattern shown in the number sequence below, what is the missing number?

   1   3   9   18   ?   72   144

   A. 27   **B.** 36   **C.** 49   **D.** 21   **E.** 63

   Answer [ ]

12. If you count from 1 to 100, how many 6s will you pass on the way?

   A. 10   **B.** 19   **C.** 20   **D.** 11   **E.** 21

   Answer [ ]

13. 50% of 350 equals?

   A. 170   **B.** 25   **C.** 175   **D.** 170   **E.** 700

   Answer [ ]

14. 75% of 1000 equals?

   A. 75   **B.** 0.75   **C.** 75000   **D.** 750   **E.** 7.5

   Answer [ ]

15. 40% of 40 equals?

A. 160   **B.** 4   **C.** 1600   **D.** 1.6   **E.** 16

Answer

16. 25% of 75 equals?

A. 18   **B.** 18.75   **C.** 18.25   **D.** 25   **E.** 17.25

Answer

17. 15% of 500 equals?

A. 75   **B.** 50   **C.** 0.75   **D.** 0.505   **E.** 750

Answer

18. 5% of 85 equals?

A. 4   **B.** 80   **C.** 4.25   **D.** 0.85   **E.** 89.25

Answer

19. 9876 – 6789 equals?

A. 3078   **B.** 3085   **C.** 783   **D.** 3086   **E.** 3087

Answer

20. 27 × 4 equals?

A. 106   **B.** 107   **C.** 108   **D.** 109   **E.** 110

Answer

21. 96 ÷ 4 equals?

A. 22   **B.** 23   **C.** 24   **D.** 25   **E.** 26

Answer

22. 8765 − 876 equals?

   A. 9887   **B.** 7888   **C.** 7890   **D.** 7998   **E.** 7889

   Answer

23. 623 + 222 equals?

   A. 840   **B.** 845   **C.** 740   **D.** 745   **E.** 940

   Answer

24. A rectangle has an area of 24 cm². The length of one side is 8 cm. What is the perimeter of the rectangle?

   A. 22 inches   **B.** 24 cm   **C.** 18 cm   **D.** 22 cm
   E. 18 inches

   Answer

25. A square has a perimeter of 36 cm. Its area is 81 cm². What is the length of one side?

   A. 9 cm   **B.** 18 cm   **C.** 9 metres   **D.** 18 metres
   E. 16 cm

   Answer

26. Which of the following is the same as 25/1000?

   A. 0.25   **B.** 0.025   **C.** 0.0025   **D.** 40   **E.** 25000

   Answer

27. Is 33 divisible by 3?

   A. Yes   **B.** No

   Answer

28. What is 49% of 1100?

   A. 535   **B.** 536   **C.** 537   **D.** 538   **E.** 539

   Answer

29. One side of a rectangle is 12 cm. If the area of the rectangle is 84 cm², what is the length of the shorter side?

A. 5 cm   **B.** 6 cm   **C.** 7 cm   **D.** 8 cm   **E.** 9 cm

Answer

30. A rectangle has an area of 8 cm². The length of one side is 2 cm. What is the perimeter?

A. 4 cm   **B.** 6 cm   **C.** 8 cm   **D.** 10 cm   **E.** None of these

Answer

Answers to the sample practice numerical test questions can be found over page.

how2become

Answers to sample practice numerical test questions

1. C	**7.** A	**13.** C	**19.** E	**25.** A
2. A	**8.** E	**14.** D	**20.** C	**26.** B
3. D	**9.** A	**15.** E	**21.** C	**27.** A
4. E	**10.** B	**16.** B	**22.** E	**28.** E
5. B	**11.** B	**17.** A	**23.** B	**29.** C
6. D	**12.** C	**18.** C	**24.** D	**30.** E

CHAPTER 10
UNDERSTANDING INFORMATION

The understanding information test is designed to assess your ability to learn and retain information. Firefighters need to be capable of learning lots of job specific information. They also need to be able to retain that information so that they can use it during training and at operational incidents. There are plenty of policies and procedures to learn and you will also need to be fully conversant with the operating manuals for your equipment and PPE.

If you can pass this test successfully then there is a good chance that you will be able to apply the same skills to the role of a firefighter.

During this test you will be presented with a written passage and it is your job to read the text carefully before answering a series of questions based on the information provided.

You may also find that the information provided is presented by video or verbally. If this is the case then you may be permitted to take notes during the presentation. After reading

the passage, your options are **True**, **False** or **Cannot say** based on the information provided.

Remember to answer the questions based solely on the information provided and do not make the mistake of assuming anything.

On the following pages are ten short passages followed by a series of questions for you to answer. Remember to base your responses *solely* on the information provided. Although some of the information within the passages relates to fire safety and firefighter procedures it should not be relied upon as an accurate source of information to prevent fires or otherwise.

Write down your answers on a blank sheet of paper.

You are allowed five minutes only per exercise. Once you have completed Part 1, move on to Part 2 of the understanding information exercises.

Understanding information – Part 1

Exercise I

Read the following passage before answering the questions below based on the information provided.

Electricity is everywhere in our homes and it is an important part of our lives. It only takes one badly wired plug to prove just how powerful it is.

The wires don't even need to touch for a spark to jump and a fire to start. You should never become complacent where electricity is concerned. Just because there's no flame doesn't mean there's no fire risk.

The major rule where fires are concerned is that you should not put people's lives at risk. Get everyone out of your home and call the Fire Service.

1. Complacency is a must where fire is concerned.

    A. True   **B.** False   **C.** Cannot say

2. Where fire is concerned people's safety is a must. You should get everyone out and call the Fire Service.

    A. True   **B.** False.   **C.** Cannot say

3. You should never put water on an electrical fire.

    A. True   **B.** False   **C.** Cannot say

Exercise 2

Read the following passage before answering the questions below based on the information provided.

Approximately two-thirds of all domestic fires are cooking related. That's a lot of fires. The kitchen is the single most dangerous place in the home.

The fact is that time and time again it's the same problems that cause the fires in kitchens up and down the UK. If you know what the problems are, the chances of having a fire in the kitchen are greatly reduced.

1. The kitchen is one of the safest places in the home.

    A. True   **B.** False   **C.** Cannot say

2. Overheated chip pans are the biggest cause of fires in the kitchen.

    A. True   **B.** False   **C.** Cannot say

3. It is the same problems that cause the fires in kitchens up and down the UK.

    A. True   **B.** False   **C.** Cannot say

Exercise 3

Read the following passage before answering the questions below based on the information provided.

You're twice as likely to die in a fire at home if you do not have a working smoke alarm. A smoke alarm is the most effective way of alerting you and your family to the dangers of fire.

This will give you precious time to escape and get out safely. They are relatively cheap, easy to get hold of and simple to fit.

However, many people who have smoke alarms are in danger too. The alarm could be in the wrong place, there may not be enough of them or the battery could be missing.

1. You are less likely to die in a fire at home if you have a working smoke alarm.

   A. True   **B.** False   **C.** Cannot say

2. Many people who have smoke alarms are still in danger.

   A. True   **B.** False   **C.** Cannot say

3. If the smoke alarm does not conform to the relevant British Standard there is the possibility that it will not work effectively in the event of a fire.

   A. True   **B.** False   **C.** Cannot say

Exercise 4

Read the following passage before answering the questions below based on the information provided.

In addition to saving life, firefighters are responsible for reducing the risk of fire and other such emergencies within the community that they serve. In order to achieve this they will visit schools in order to educate children

on how to prevent fires from occurring in the first place, liaise with different stakeholders within the community to identify who is at risk from fire, and also work with the other emergency services to look for ways to reduce problem incidents such as road traffic collisions. The firefighter's role, therefore, is extremely varied and it is not purely focused on saving life.

1. The firefighter's role is focused purely on saving life.

   A. True   **B.** False   **C.** Cannot say

2. Firefighters will educate school children on why they shouldn't make hoax calls.

   A. True   **B.** False   **C.** Cannot say

3. In order to look for ways to reduce problem incidents such as road traffic collisions the Fire Service will work with other emergency services.

   A. True   **B.** False   **C.** Cannot say

Exercise 5

Read the following passage before answering the questions below based on the information provided.

Health and Safety is a very important aspect of a firefighter's role. It is the responsibility of a firefighter to keep themselves and their work colleagues safe at all times.

As part of their role they will carry out a dynamic risk assessment during operational incidents. As part of the dynamic risk assessment process, firefighters will first evaluate the risks before selecting a safe system of work. Once they have selected the appropriate safe system of work they will need to decide whether the risks are proportional to the benefits. If the risks are proportional to the benefits then they will proceed with the task.

If the risks are not proportional then they will look to introduce additional control measures before proceeding.

1. Firefighters carry out a dynamic risk assessment during operational incidents.

   A. True   **B.** False   **C.** Cannot say

2. Part of the dynamic risk assessment process involves deciding whether the risks are proportional to the benefits.

   A. True   **B.** False   **C.** Cannot say

3. If the risks are not proportional then firefighters will not look to introduce additional control measures before proceeding.

   A. True   **B.** False   **C.** Cannot say

Exercise 6

Read the following passage before answering the questions below based on the information provided.

Firefighters are often called upon to tackle various emergency incidents ranging from house fires, care fires, chemical incidents and even animals stuck in rivers or mud. Each situation will require a different level of skill but at all times they need to remain calm, composed and focused on the task in hand. A sensitive approach is always required when dealing with members of the public who may be distressed, shocked and confused.

In order to prepare for each emergency incident, firefighters will carry out a large amount or training that is as close to the real thing as possible. For example, they will simulate a road traffic collision so that they can test their skills, equipment and procedures in a safe and controlled environment.

In order to ensure that their personal protective equipment and operational equipment is ready for use at all times,

they will carry out a taking-over routine at every change of shift. In addition to examining their PPE and operational equipment for defects this taking-over routine will allow them to familiarise themselves with their most important items of equipment.

1. Taking-over routines are always carried out at the end of a firefighter's shift.

    A. True   **B.** False   **C.** Cannot say

2. Personal Protective Equipment includes a helmet and fire gloves.

    A. True   **B.** False   **C.** Cannot say

3. A sensitive approach is always required when dealing with members of the public who may be distressed, shocked and confused.

    A. True   **B.** False   **C.** Cannot say

Exercise 7

Read the following passage before answering the questions below based on the information provided.

As a firefighter you will be expected to undertake a programme of continuous professional development (CPD).

CPD is a continuous learning and development process that will last the firefighter's entire career. CPD can be achieved by attending lectures, taking part in exercises and conducting practical training sessions in order to maintain the high competence levels required to be a firefighter.

Firefighters are expected to take responsibility for developing their own skills and for ensuring that their fitness levels are maintained as the work can be demanding, both physically and mentally.

1. In order to maintain their high levels of competencies firefighters must embark on a development process that is called Continuous Professional Development.

   A. True   **B.** False   **C.** Cannot say

2. The responsibility for developing a firefighter's own skills rests with the line manager.

   A. True   **B.** False   **C.** Cannot say

3. The initial firefighter training course forms part of the Continuous Professional Development process.

   A. True   **B.** False   **C.** Cannot say

Exercise 8

Read the following passage before answering the questions below based on the information provided.

Many fire services are now offering a free home fire safety visit to people who live within the area of the fire station. The service itself is designed to provide the homeowner with information that makes them aware of the potential risks from fire within their home. This service is proving to be more and more popular among homeowners and it has also contributed significantly to the reduction of accidental property fires and deaths.

The service itself may be carried out by operational fire crews or by a designated Community Safety team. In addition to identifying the potential risks, the service will also inform the homeowner what they need to do in the event of a fire. It will also provide them with an escape plan so they can get out safely if a fire were to occur in the home.

1. Part of an escape plan is to make sure you know where your front door keys are kept, especially at night.

   A. True   **B.** False   **C.** Cannot say

2. For those people who live within the area of the fire station a home fire safety check is available at a relatively cheap cost.

   A. True   **B.** False   **C.** Cannot say

3. The home fire safety check service itself is designed to provide the homeowner with information that makes them aware of the potential risks from fire within their home.

   A. True   **B.** False   **C.** Cannot say

Exercise 9

Read the following passage before answering the questions below based on the information provided.

When cooking at home it is important to take extra care. For example, you could be frying some food and become distracted by the door bell or phone ringing. Remember to turn off the heat before leaving the kitchen unattended.

You should also ensure that you are not wearing any loose or baggy clothing as this can easily catch fire. While cooking it is essential that you keep all electrical leads, towels and other combustible items away from the heat source.

If you are cooking in the kitchen then make sure your children are supervised outside of the kitchen area. Never leave children alone in the kitchen. You must also make sure that you keep all matches, lighters and other sources of ignition out of a child's reach, even when you are not cooking. There have been many incidents when children have managed to reach unattended ignition sources in the kitchen. Make sure they are locked away safely at all times.

1. It is acceptable to leave children unattended in the kitchen area.

   A. True   **B.** False   **C.** Cannot say

2. You should ensure that you keep the grill, hob and oven clean and free from grease to reduce the risk of fire.

   A. True   **B.** False   **C.** Cannot say

3. There have been many incidents when children have used ignition sources from the kitchen to start fires.

   A. True   **B.** False   **C.** Cannot say

Exercise IO

Read the following passage before answering the questions below based on the information provided.

Business owners should carry out regular fire drills depending on the nature of their premises and business. At the very least this process should be carried out once a year. The most effective way to conduct a fire drill is when nobody in the premises is expecting it. This will allow you to gauge exactly how your employers would react in a real-life emergency situation.

In order to get the most out of the fire drill, everyone must take part. Once you have completed the fire drill you should record the result in your fire log book. In addition to carrying out fire drills, you must provide all employees with instruction and training so that they know what to do in the event of a fire.

1. At the very least fire drills should be carried out twice a year.

   A. True   **B.** False   **C.** Cannot say

2. Everyone must take part in the fire drill in order for it to be effective.

   A. True   **B.** False   **C.** Cannot say

3. In addition to carrying out fire drills, business owners must provide all employees with instruction and training so that they know what to do in the event of a fire.

   A. True   **B.** False   **C.** Cannot say

Answers to understanding information – Part 1

Exercise 1

1. B

2. A

3. C

Exercise 2

1. B

2. C

3. A

Exercise 3

1. A

2. A

3. C

Exercise 4

1. B

2. C

3. A

Exercise 5

1. A

2. A

3. B

Exercise 6

1. B

2. C

3. A

Exercise 7
1. A

2. B

3. C

Exercise 8
1. C

2. B

3. A

Exercise 9
1. B

2. C

3. C

Exercise 10
1. B

2. A

3. A

Now that you have attempted Part 1, take a look at 'Understanding information – Part 2.

Understanding information – Part 2

These exercises are slightly harder than the exercises in Part 1 and will push your skills even further. Please note that the subjects used in these sample tests are not Fire Service related and are different from the type of test that you will be required to sit on the day. However, they are a great way to improve your ability at answering the questions in this type of test.

There are five exercises in this section and you have a total of 15 minutes to complete all of them.

Exercise I

Car A is red in colour and has 11 months left on the current MOT. The tax is due in 4 months' time. The car has a full service history and has completed 34,000 miles. The car has had three owners.

Car B is black in colour and has a full 12 months' MOT. The tax is not due for another 12 months. The car has completed 3,445 miles and has had only one owner. There is a full service history with the car.

Car C is red in colour and has no tax. The MOT is due to run out in 12 weeks' time and it has no service history. The speedometer reading is 134,000 miles and the car has had a total of 11 owners.

Car D is black in colour and has 11 months left on the current MOT. The tax is due in 6 months' time. The car has no service history and has completed 34,000 miles. The car has had only one owner.

Car E is red in colour and has 7 months' tax. The MOT runs out in 7 months' time. The car has a partial service history and has completed 97,000 miles. It has had a total of four owners.

Questions

1. You want a car that is red in colour and has a full service history with less than 100,000 miles. Which car do you choose?

A.	**B.**	**C.**	**D.**	**E.**
Car A	Car B	Car C	Car D	Car E

2. You want a car that has more than 6 months' tax. You are not concerned about the colour but you also want 12 months' MOT. Which car do you choose?

A.	**B.**	**C.**	**D.**	**E.**
Car A	Car B	Car C	Car D	Car E

3. You want a car that is red in colour and has had no more than four owners. You want a minimum of 6 months' tax. The mileage is irrelevant but you do want at least 7 months' MOT. Which car do you choose?

A.   **B.**   **C.**   **D.**   **E.**

Car A   Car B   Car C   Car D   Car E

Exercise 2

Flight A outbound leaves at 8a.m. and arrives at 1p.m. The cost of the flight is £69 but this does not include a meal or refreshments. The return flight departs at 3a.m. and arrives at its destination at 8a.m.

Flight B outbound leaves at 3p.m. and arrives at 8p.m. The cost of the flight is £97 and this includes a meal and refreshments. The return flight departs at 1p.m. and arrives at its destination at 5p.m.

Flight C outbound leaves at 4p.m. and arrives at 10p.m. The cost of the flight is £70 but this does not include a meal or refreshments. The return flight departs at 10a.m. and arrives at its destination at 4p.m.

Flight D outbound leaves at midnight and arrives at 3a.m. The cost of the flight is £105, which does include a meal and refreshments. The return flight departs at 3p.m. and arrives at 6p.m.

Flight E outbound leaves at 5a.m. and arrives at 12 noon. The cost of the flight is £39, which includes a meal and refreshments. The return flight departs at 5p.m. and arrives at its destination at midnight.

Questions

1. You want a flight where the outbound flight arrives before 2p.m. on the day of departure. You don't want to pay any more than £50. Which flight do you choose?

    A.   **B.**   **C.**   **D.**   **E.**

    Flight A   Flight B   Flight C   Flight D   Flight E

2. You don't want to pay any more than £100 for the flight. You want a meal and the outbound departure time must be in the afternoon. Which flight do you choose?

    A.   **B.**   **C.**   **D.**   **E.**

    Flight A   Flight B   Flight C   Flight D   Flight E

3. You want a return flight that departs in the afternoon between 12 noon and 6p.m. The cost of the flight must be below £100 and you do want a meal. The return flight must arrive at your destination before 6p.m. Which flight do you choose?

    A.   **B.**   **C.**   **D.**   **E.**

    Flight A   Flight B   Flight C   Flight D   Flight E

Exercise 3

Janet and Steve have been married for 27 years. They have a daughter called Jessica who is 25 years old. They all want to go on holiday together but cannot make up their minds where to go.

Janet's first choice would be somewhere hot and sunny abroad. Her second choice would be somewhere in their home country that involves a sporting activity. She does not like hill climbing or walking holidays but her third choice would be a skiing holiday.

Steve's first choice would be a walking holiday in the hills somewhere in their home country and his second choice would be a sunny holiday abroad. He does not enjoy skiing.

Jessica's first choice would be a skiing holiday and her second choice would be a sunny holiday abroad. Jessica's third choice would be a walking holiday in the hills of their home country.

Questions

1. Which holiday are all the family members most likely to go on together?

    A. Skiing
    B. Walking
    C. Sunny holiday abroad
    D. Sporting activity holiday
    E. Cannot say

2. If Steve and Jessica were to go on holiday together where would they be most likely to go?

    A. Sunny holiday abroad
    B. Skiing
    C. Cannot say
    D. Sporting activity holiday
    E. Walking

3. Which holiday are Janet and Steve most likely to go on together?

    A. Cannot say
    B. Walking
    C. Sporting activity holiday
    D. Skiing
    E. Sunny holiday abroad

Exercise 4

Barry and Bill work at their local supermarket in the town of Whiteham. Barry works every day except Wednesdays. The supermarket is run by Barry's brother Elliot who is married to Sarah.

Sarah and Elliot have two children called Marcus and Michelle who are both 7 years old and they live in the road adjacent to the supermarket. Barry lives in a town called Redford, which is 7 miles from Whiteham. Bill's girlfriend Maria works in a factory in her hometown of Brownhaven. The town of Redford is 4 miles from Whiteham and 6 miles from the seaside town of Tenford. Sarah and Elliot take their children on holiday to Tenford twice a year and Barry usually gives them a lift in his car.

Barry's mum lives in Tenford and he tries to visit her once a week at 2p.m. when he is not working.

Questions

1. Which town does Elliot live in?

    A. Redford
    B. Whiteham
    C. Brownhaven
    D. Tenford
    E. Cannot say

2. On which day of the week does Barry visit his mother?

    A. Cannot say
    B. Monday
    C. Tuesday
    D. Wednesday
    E. Thursday

3. Bill and Maria live together in Brownhaven.

    A. True
    B. False
    C. Cannot say

Exercise 5

Flat A is located in a town. It is 12 miles from the nearest train station. It has two bedrooms and is located on the ground

floor. The monthly rental is £450 and the council tax is £50 per month. The lease is for 6 months.

Flat B is located in the city centre and is 2 miles from the nearest train station. It is located on the third floor. The monthly rental is £600 and the council tax is £130 per month. The lease is for 6 months and it has three bedrooms.

Flat C is located in the city centre and is 3 miles from the nearest train station. It is located on the first floor and has one bedroom. The monthly rental is £550 and the council tax is £100 per month. The lease is for 12 months.

Flat D is located in a town. The monthly rental is £395 per month and the council tax is £100 per month. It is located on the ground floor and the lease is for 6 months. It is 18 miles from the nearest train station. The flat has two bedrooms.

Flat E is located in a village and is 12 miles from the nearest train station. It has three bedrooms and is located on the second floor. The monthly rental is £375 and the council tax is £62.

Questions

1. You want a flat that is within 10 miles of the nearest train station and is located on the first floor or lower. The combined monthly rent/council tax bill must be no greater than £600. Which flat do you choose?

    A. Flat A
    B. Flat B
    C. Flat C
    D. Flat D
    E. None of the above

2. You want a flat that has at least two bedrooms and has a combined monthly rent/council tax bill that does not exceed £450. Which flat do you choose?

   A. Flat A
   B. Flat B
   C. Flat C
   D. Flat D
   E. Flat E

3. You want a flat that has a combined monthly rent/council tax bill that is not in excess of £600, is within 20 miles of the nearest train station and has a lease of at least 6 months. Which flat do you choose?

   A. Flat A
   B. Flat B
   C. Flat A, D or E
   D. Flat A or E
   E. Flat C or D

Answers to understanding information – Part 2

Exercise 1	**Exercise 4**
1. A	**1.** B
2. B	**2.** D
3. E	**3.** C

Exercise 2	**Exercise 5**
1. E	**1.** E
2. B	**2.** E
3. B	**3.** C

Exercise 3
1. C

2. A

3. E

Tips for Passing the Understanding Information Test

- Read the information quickly before looking at the question. Once you understand the question you may decide to 'scan' the information again in order to search for the answer. Don't spend too long reading the information.

- A great way to prepare for this type of test is to read newspaper and magazine articles. After reading an article, write down as much information as you can about the piece without referring to it.

- Finally, you may wish to purchase additional psychometric testing booklets from www.how2become.co.uk.

THE FIREFIGHTER
INTERVIEW

CHAPTER II
PREPARING FOR THE INTERVIEW

Each stage of the application process is very important but you will probably find that this is the one stage that causes you the most nerves. In fact, if you don't feel nervous leading up to and during your interview, then you are less likely to perform to your maximum capability.

If you have reached this stage of the selection process then the Fire Service is interested in employing you and its representatives will want to meet you face to face in order to see what you are like as a person, and also whether you really do have the skills required to become a firefighter.

This section will provide you with essential tips on the interview stage including preparation and sample questions.

Before I provide you with a number of sample interview questions and tips, let's go back to our 'plan'. If I was preparing for the firefighter interview today, I would first ask myself the following two questions:

Q1. What areas will the Fire Service interview panel assess me on during the interview?

Q2. What would the interview panel expect to see from successful interview candidates?

Once again, I write down my perceived answers to these questions, and I get the following responses:

A1. The members of the panel will probably ask me questions that are based around the firefighter Personal Qualities and Attributes. They will require me to provide 'specific' examples of where I already have experience in each of the PQA areas. They will also want to know why I want to become a firefighter and, in particular, why I want to join their Fire Service. They may also want to know how I have prepared for the selection process and what qualities I believe I have that will be relevant to the role.

A2. They would expect successful candidates to provide specific examples that relate to the PQA related questions. They would also expect my responses to the interview questions to be concise, relevant, well-structured and in a logical sequence. They would also want to see that I have put a large amount of work into my application and that I am genuinely motivated and committed to becoming a firefighter within their organisation. They will want to see that I have gone out of my way to find out about the role of a firefighter, including the proactive side of the role.

Now that I have my two answers I will set out another simple plan that dictates exactly what I am going to do. In this particular case it will look something like this:

- I will learn the PQAs thoroughly and I will think of specific examples where I can match each and every one of them. I will use the STAR method when constructing my responses to the interview questions which will allow

me to put them across in a concise and logical manner. I will think of genuine reasons why I want to become a firefighter and I will make sure that I can provide good reasons as to why I want to join their particular Fire Service. I will also write down exactly what I have done to prepare for the selection process and also the qualities I believe I possess that would be suited to the role.

- I will visit my local fire station and speak to the firefighters about their role. I will also visit the website of the Fire Service I am applying to join and learn about the proactive side to the job in addition to the reactive side.

Now that you have your plan of action we can move on to the interview tips and questions. Any potential employee must demonstrate that he/she has the ability to perform the role expected of him/her. During the interview you will need to demonstrate that you have the potential to become a firefighter and this is what the panel will be looking for.

You will have thoroughly read this guide and learnt a tremendous amount about the Fire Service and what the role of the firefighter actually involves. Remember everything you have learnt so far and use the sample question templates within this guide to help you to construct your own responses.

Your preparation should start weeks before your interview date, not the night before.

About the firefighter interview

The interview is usually a relatively informal affair that is designed to assess your knowledge of the firefighter's role and, in particular, how you can meet the Personal Qualities and Attributes that are relevant to the role. While the majority of questions are usually based around the PQAs, you should also prepare for the more generic type of interview questions that are contained within this guide.

> **Top Tip**
>
> Read and understand the Firefighter Personal Qualities and Attributes before you attend the interview and be ready to provide specific examples of where your skills meet each one.

How long will the interview last?

The interview should last no longer than one hour. Usually between 45 and 50 minutes is the norm, but this will depend on the length of your responses.

What should I wear to the interview?

You will not normally be assessed on your dress but I strongly advise that you wear a formal outfit such as a suit. Make sure your shoes are clean and polished and do not wear white socks or socks with cartoon characters on them!

What is the purpose of the interview?

The main purpose of the interview is to talk about you and your interest in becoming a firefighter, and then to look at some areas of your experience in more detail.

Is everyone asked the same set of questions?

Yes they are. This is so that the process is fair and everyone gets the same chance.

How many people will be on the panel?

This depends on the service you are applying to join. There could be two, three or even four people on the panel. They could be a mix of uniformed personnel and non-uniformed personnel. There will usually be someone on the panel from the Human Resources department to ensure the interview is fair and consistent.

How will the interview commence?

The panel will ask you to sit down and introduce themselves to you. There will be a glass of water on the table in front of you and you will be asked to make yourself comfortable. While it is all right to make yourself feel comfortable, do remember that you are being assessed so make sure you watch your interview technique.

The panel will then explain the purpose of the interview to you. They will state that they are going to ask you for specific examples of what you have done in different situations. It is all right to draw from examples from home, work, school, college or hobbies. It is advisable that you draw from a variety of different experiences.

How will I be assessed?

You will normally be assessed against the Personal Qualities and Attributes that are relevant to the role of a firefighter, but this will very much depend on the Fire Service that you are applying to join.

The key assessment areas are as follows:

- Commitment to excellence
- Commitment to development
- Commitment to diversity and integrity (this area carries the most importance)
- Communicating effectively

> **Top Tip**
>
> Do not use jargon. Make sure you communicate in language the panel can understand!

Before you get into the formal assessment questions, the interview panel will more often than not ask you a set

of 'warm-up' questions. These will last approximately ten minutes and it is your chance to get off on the right foot.

What warm-up questions will I be asked?

How was your journey here today?
Try to answer this question more than just 'okay' or 'good'. Use the warm-up questions as a chance to communicate with the panel. For example:

The journey was very good thank you. Before I came for the interview today I planned my route and checked on the news to see if there were any traffic problems or hold-ups that could have delayed my travel time. I managed to avoid a tailback on the motorway, so thankfully the journey was very relaxing.

What interests you about becoming a firefighter?
This is a great opportunity to get the interview going along the right lines! The Fire Service offers teamwork, opportunities to help and support the community and the chance to work in a diverse workforce. Be positive in your response and think carefully about the role of a firefighter.

How did you hear about the fact that we are recruiting?
Try to show here that you are keen and have been keeping in touch with your local fire station and the service's website to check for recruitment updates, keeping your eye on the local paper, and so on.

What steps have you taken to find out more about the role of a firefighter?
Again, maybe you have visited the local fire station, visited their website, attended a course, bought and studied a book or DVD.

Can you tell me about some of your interests or hobbies?

Tell the panel something about you that is interesting. Maybe you play sports or outdoor activities. Even if you just enjoy walking to keep fit, this is still positive.

You could be asked a whole host of warm-up questions. Just make sure you provide positive answers and use the questions as an opportunity to get into 'interview mode'!

Once the warm-up questions are complete, the interviewer may take a drink of water at this point. You may also take a drink of water and compose yourself, ready for the formal interview questions. You will then be informed that you are moving into the formal part of the interview. A member of the panel will say something along the lines of 'OK, we are now moving on to the first PQA, which will last approximately ten minutes'.

Please note – the PQA questions can come in any order.

The most important piece of advice I can give you

Throughout this book I have made reference to the Firefighter Personal Qualities and Attributes. During the interview there is a strong possibility that you could be asked questions relating to these.

If I were preparing for the firefighter interview right now, I would take each PQA individually and prepare a detailed response setting out where I meet the requirements of the PQA. Your response to each question that relates to the PQAs must be 'specific' in nature. This means that you must provide an example of where you have already demonstrated the skills that are required under the PQA. Do not fall into the trap of providing a 'generic' response that details what you 'would do' if the situation arose.

Structure your responses in a logical and concise manner. The way to achieve this is to use the 'STAR' method of interview question response construction:

Situation

Start off your response to the interview question by explaining what the 'situation' was and who was involved.

Task

Once you have detailed the situation, explain what the 'task' was, or what needed to be done.

Action

Now explain what 'action' you took, and what action others took. Also explain why you took this particular course of action.

Result

Then explain what the outcome or 'result' was following your actions and those of others. Try to demonstrate in your response that the result was positive because of the action you took.

Finally, explain to the panel what you would do differently if the same situation arose again. It is good to be reflective at the end of your responses. This demonstrates a level of maturity and it will also show the panel that you are willing to learn from every experience.

CHAPTER 12
SAMPLE INTERVIEW QUESTIONS

The different types of interview question

Basically there are two different types of interview question that you could be asked. I will now explain each of them and what they mean.

Generic questions about you and your knowledge of the Fire Service and the firefighter's role

Generic questions can be in any format. There is no particular structure to this type of question but they are generally far easier to respond to. Examples of generic questions would include:

- Why do you want to become a firefighter?

- What has attracted you to this Fire Service in particular?

- What have you learnt about the role of a firefighter?

- Why should we choose you against the other applicants?

Generic questions are becoming less and less popular during the firefighter interview and the majority of fire services are now using 'PQA' based questions. However, it is still important to prepare for the generic type of questions.

PQA questions

This type of question is becoming more and more popular during the firefighter interview and you should certainly concentrate the majority of your preparation in this area. The personal qualities and attributes are generally the 'blueprint' for the role of a firefighter. The interview panel will want to know whether you already have these skills and that you can give examples to demonstrate your use of them in your responses to the questions.

Within this section of the guide I will provide you with a large number of sample interview questions that have been used during firefighter selection interviews. Having asked some of these questions myself of potential candidates, I will also provide brief details on what I believe makes a strong response, and what I believe makes a weak one.

While you will not be asked every question that follows, they will all give you a great hand during your preparation and I strongly recommend you prepare a response for each of them. Plenty of hard work and determination is needed here, so be prepared to knuckle down and put in the effort.

Questions based around the Personal Qualities

The first PQA deals with working with others and will show the extent to which you work effectively with other people in the community.

Sample PQA question I

Tell me about a time when you have contributed to the effective working of a team.

How to structure your response:

- What was the size and purpose of the team?

- Who else was in the team?

- What was YOUR role in the team? (Explain your exact role)

- What did you personally do to help make the team effective?

- What was the result?

Strong response

To make your response strong you need to provide specific details of where you have worked with others effectively, and more importantly where YOU have contributed to the team.

Think of an example where there was a problem within a team and where you volunteered to make the team work more efficiently. It is better to say that you identified there was a problem within the team rather than that you were asked to do something by your manager or supervisor.

Make your response concise and logical.

Weak response

Those candidates who fail to provide a specific example will provide weak answers. Do not fall into the trap of saying 'what you would do' if this type of situation arose.

Sample PQA question 2

Tell me about a time when you helped someone who was distressed or in need of support.

How to structure your response:

- What was the situation?

- Why did you provide the help? (Whether you were approached or you volunteered – TIP: It is better to say you volunteered!)
- What did you do to support the individual?
- What specifically did you do or say?
- What was the result?

Strong response

Again, make sure you provide a specific example of where you have helped someone who was in distress or who needed your support. Provide an example where the outcome was a positive one as a result of your actions. If the situation was one that involved potentially dangerous surroundings (such as a car accident), did you consider the safety aspect and did you carry out a risk assessment of the scene?

Weak response

Candidates who provide a weak response will be generic in their answering. The outcome of the situation will generally not be a positive one.

The next PQA deals with commitment to excellence. This will show how you would display a conscientious and proactive approach to work to achieve and maintain excellent standards.

Sample PQA question 3

Tell me about a time when you had to follow clear instructions or rules in order to complete a task.

How to structure your response:

- What was the work you were doing?
- What were the rules or instructions that you had to follow?
- What did you do to complete the work as directed?
- What was the result?
- How did you feel about completing the task in this way?

Strong response

The Fire Service strives for excellence in everything it does. Therefore it is crucial that you provide a response that demonstrates you too can deliver excellence and maintain high standards. Try to think of a situation, either at work or otherwise, where you have achieved this. Make your response specific in nature. If you have had to follow specific instructions, rules or procedures then this is a good thing to tell the panel.

Weak response

Weak responses are generic in nature and usually focus on a candidate's own views on how a task should be achieved, rather than in line with a company's or organisation's policies and procedures. The candidate will display a lack of motivation in relation to following clear instructions or rules.

Sample PQA question 4

Tell me about a time when you sought to improve the way that you or others do things.

How to structure your answer:

- What was the improvement that you made?

- What prompted this change?

- What did you personally do to ensure that the change was successful?

- What was the result?

Strong response

Part of the firefighter's role includes continuous improvement and being able to adapt to change. Stronger performing candidates are able to provide a response that demonstrates a voluntary willingness to improve or change the way they do things.

Weak response

Candidates who are unable to identify where improvements are needed will generally provide weak responses. Once again the response will be generic in nature and lack any substance or specific evidence.

The next PQA deals with commitment to development. This will show your commitment and ability to develop yourself and others.

Sample PQA question 5

Tell me about a time when you have taken it upon yourself to learn a new skill or develop an existing one.

How to structure your response:

- What skill did you learn or develop?

- What prompted this development?

- When did this learning or development occur or take place?

- How did you go about learning or developing this skill?

- What was the result?

- How has this skill helped you since then?

Strong response

Firefighters are required to learn new skills every week. They will attend ongoing training courses and they will also read up on new procedures and policies. In order to maintain a high level of professionalism, firefighters must be committed to continuous development. Think of an occasion when you have learnt a new skill, or where you have taken it upon yourself to develop your knowledge or experience in a particular subject. Follow the above structure format to create a strong response.

Weak response

Those candidates who have taken on any new development or learning will be unable to provide a strong response. They will provide a response where they were told to learn a new skill, rather than taking it upon themselves. There will be no structure to their learning or development and they will display a lack of motivation when learning.

Sample PQA question 6

Tell me about a time when you changed how you did something in response to feedback from someone else.

How to structure your response:

* What did you need to develop?

* What feedback did you receive and from whom?

* What steps did you take to improve yourself or someone else?

* What did you specifically say or do?

* What was the result?

Strong response

Firefighters receive feedback from their supervisory managers on a regular basis. In their quest to continually improve, the Fire Service will invest time, finances and resources into your development. Part of the learning process includes being able to accept feedback and also being able to improve as a result of it.

Strongly performing candidates will be able to provide a specific example of where they have taken feedback from an employer or otherwise, and used it to improve themselves.

Weak response

Those candidates who are unable to accept feedback from others and change as a result will generally provide a weak response to this type of question. They will fail to grasp the importance of feedback and in particular where it lies in relation to continuous improvement. Their response will be generic in nature and there will be no real substance or detail to their answer.

The final PQA deals with commitment to diversity and integrity. The questions ask how you understand and respect other people's values and how you would adopt a fair and ethical approach to others. Diversity means the differences that exist between people, such as gender, age, ethnic background, religion, social background.

Sample PQA question 7

Describe a time when you have helped to support diversity in a team, school, college or organisation.

How to structure your response:

- What was the situation?

- What prompted the situation?

- What were the diversity issues?

- What steps did you take to support others from diverse backgrounds?

- What specifically did you say or do?

- What was the result?

Strong response

This type of question is difficult to respond to, especially if you have little or no experience in this area. However, strongly performing candidates will be able to provide clear details and examples of where they have supported diversity in a given situation. Their response will be specific in nature and

it will clearly indicate to the panel that they are serious about this important subject.

Weak response
Weak responses are generic in nature and they fail to answer the question that is being asked. Many candidates are unable to provide a specific response to this type of question.

Sample PQA question 8

Tell me about a time when you noticed a member of your team or group behaving in a manner which was inconsistent with the team's, group's, or organisation's values.

How to structure your answer:

- What was the situation?
- How was the behaviour inconsistent with the team's or organisation's values?
- Why were the colleagues behaving in that way?
- What did you say or do when you noticed this behaviour?
- What difficulties did you face?
- What was the result?

Strong response
Firefighters need to have the confidence and ability to challenge unacceptable behaviour while at work. In order to understand what unacceptable behaviour is, you first need to know what the values of the organisation are. Candidates who provide a strong response will have a clear understanding of an organisation's values and also how to tackle unacceptable behaviour in the correct manner.

Weak response
Weak responses are generally where a candidate is unaware of the importance of an organisation's values and how they

impact on the needs of a team or group. They will not have the confidence to challenge inappropriate behaviour and they will turn a blind eye whenever possible. Their response will lack structure and it will be generic in nature.

Sample PQA question 9

Tell me about a time when you made a mistake that had a knock-on effect on other people?

How to structure your answer:

• What were the circumstances?

• What was the mistake?

• How did the mistake affect others?

• What did you do or say when you noticed your mistake?

• What was the outcome?

• What would you do differently next time?

Strong response
We all make mistakes from time to time but what is important is what you do after the mistake. Strongly performing candidates will provide honest details about the mistake they made and also how they improved as a result of it. They will also provide details of how they reflected on their performance and how they evaluated their actions with a view to improve.

Weak response
Candidates who provide a weak response will state that they are perfect and that they never make mistakes. Their response will not provide an example of where a genuine mistake has been made and what they did specifically to learn from it.

Tips for Answering the PQA Interview Questions

- It is always best to say if you had to ask for advice or consulted someone on how you were dealing with a problem.

- Remember that the questions provided in this section are only samples based around the PQAs. You could be asked an interview question that is different from those above, but the questions will always be based around the PQAs. If you prepare a number of different scenarios based around the firefighter PQAs then you won't go far wrong.

- It is always positive to say whether you would have done something differently second time around if a situation occurred again, because you felt you could have done it better.

- Evaluating and reflecting on your actions is very good; you are marked on this but interviewers are not allowed to ask you, unfortunately. This will get you more points.

- It is important for your sake that you choose a number of different situations. Therefore we advise that you write down examples from your experience before you attend the interview. Always have more than one, that way you will take the pressure off yourself to remember them all.

- You are not permitted to take notes into the interview with you but it is advisable that you write down your responses during your preparation – this will help you to remember them!

Generic questions based around the firefighter's role and your knowledge of the Fire Service

Within this section I have provided a number of generic questions that you may be asked during your firefighter interview. Do not rely on the questions to come up during your interview but rather use them as a preparation tool only.

It is a good idea to practise for interviews with a friend or relative. Set up a room as you'd expect to find it in an interview and get the person to ask you questions. At the end of the mock interview ask them for feedback on how they thought you performed.

Following the initial list of questions, I have supplied explanations to some of the questions and a sample response to show how the question might be answered. Please remember that the responses are for guidance purposes only. Your responses should be based on your own individual skills, knowledge and experience.

Sample generic questions

- **Q:** Why have you applied to join the Fire Service and what do you have to offer?

- **Q:** What do you understand about the role of a firefighter?

- **Q:** What is Community Fire Safety?

- **Q:** If a member of the public asked you how to call the Fire Service, what advice would you give them?

- **Q:** Do you have any experience of working as a team member?

- **Q:** Do you have any experience of working within the community?

- **Q:** What do you understand by the term diversity?

Q: What do you understand about the term Health and Safety and who is responsible for it?

Q: What do you understand about the term Equality and Fairness?

Q: If you witnessed a member of your team being bullied or harassed at work, what action would you take and why?

Q: What would be your reaction if someone you were working with was acting in an offensive manner? (Racially or sexually)

Q: What qualities do you possess that would be of benefit to the Fire Service?

Q: Can you tell me a time when you have made a bad decision in your life and how you dealt with it?

Q: What would you do if you witnessed a friend in the Fire Service stealing?

Q: What are the current Community Fire Safety activities of this Fire and Rescue Service?

Q: How do you keep yourself fit and why do you think fitness is important to the role of a firefighter?

Q: Have you ever had any experience of taking responsibility?

Q: What do you think are the important elements of communicating with different groups of people?

Q: What qualities and attributes do you think a firefighter should have?

Q: How would you react to an angry member of the public while attending a fire?

Q: Have you ever had to deal with an emergency and if so what did you do and why?

Q: Who is the Brigade Manager/Chief Executive of this organisation?

Q: The role of a firefighter involves working long and unsociable hours. How do you think you would cope with this?

Q: What types of operational incidents do you think the Fire Service attends?

Q: How do you think you would cope when dealing with casualties at incidents?

Q: How do you deal with stress?

Q: What are your strengths?

Q: What are your weaknesses?

Q: Can you give any examples of where you have had to carry out work of a practical nature?

Q: Part of a firefighter's role is to carry out routine tasks such as cleaning of equipment and maintenance. How do you think you would cope with this element of the job?

Q: If you overheard some information that related to a work colleague committing a criminal offence, what would your reaction be?

Q: How many fire stations are there within this Fire and Rescue Service?

Q: What do you understand about the term 'Integrated Risk Management Plan'? (NOTE – This can be found on the majority of Fire and Rescue websites.)

Q: What do you know about the structure of this Fire Service?

Q: How many fire stations are there in the county?

Q: How would you feel about working with a gay or lesbian firefighter?

Q: On your way to work one morning you witness a car accident. What would you do and why?

Q: Do you currently have any responsibilities either at home or at work?

Q: How do you arrive at making difficult decisions?

Q: What experience do you have in communicating with the general public?

Q: How do you respond to pressure?

Q: Do you have any questions for the panel?

Sample generic interview question I

Why have you applied to join the Fire Service and what do you have to offer?

This question is a common one among Fire Service interview panels and one that you should prepare for. The question may be asked in a variety of different forms, but an explanation of why you have applied and what you have to offer is something that the panel will want to hear. When answering this type of question, remember to focus your response on the role of the firefighter and how you are suited to it.

The question may be worded in a way that asks you why you want to join their particular Fire and Rescue Service. If this is the case, you are advised to respond with an answer that reflects the positive aspects of that particular Fire Service.

The following is a sample response to this type of question. Once you have read the response, use it as a guide to help you construct your own answer.

Generic interview question 1 – sample response

Why have you applied to join the Fire Service and what do you have to offer?

Joining the Fire Service is something that I have wanted to do for many years now and I have been preparing for the selection process for some time. I believe that I would enjoy working in a community-focused service where the priority is helping other people, both through preventive work and reactive operational work.

Having researched the Fire Service extensively, I have been impressed and attracted to the shift from predominantly reactive work to prevention work in terms of Community Fire Safety. I enjoy learning new skills and keeping up to date with procedures and policies, and believe the Fire Service would be a career that I would be very much suited to.

I am a caring person who is comfortable working with people, regardless of their background, age, sexuality or gender. I keep myself physically fit and understand that this is an important aspect of the firefighter's role. I want to become a firefighter with this Fire and Rescue Service because I believe I can make a positive difference to the team. I am enthusiastic, motivated, focused and driven and would love to work for a professional service that has such high standards.

Sample generic interview question 2

What do you understand about the role of a firefighter?

Once again, this is a common question used by UK Fire and Rescue Services. The question is used to test your knowledge of the firefighter's role.

Many people will just respond with an answer that solely relates to the operational aspect of the role. Such a response will not be adequate to attract high marks. Remember to

make reference to the Personal Qualities and Attributes (PQAs) that are applicable to the firefighter's role.

Focus your response around the PQAs and the diverse role of the modern-day firefighter. Take a look at the following sample response before creating your own based on your own skills, knowledge and experience.

Generic interview question 2 – sample response

What do you understand about the role of a firefighter?

The two main areas of the firefighter's role are responding to incidents as and when they arise, and also Community Fire Safety work, which involves looking for ways to reduce incidents. I understand that the role is based around the Personal Qualities and Attributes for the firefighter. This includes a commitment to diversity and integrity and also being open to change.

The Fire Service is a continually changing and improving service and it is important that firefighters embrace this. A firefighter must have the confidence and resilience to deal with highly stressful situations and be capable of working with all people, regardless of age, sexuality, gender or background.

Because firefighters carry out so much community work, they have to be effective communicators and be capable of solving problems as and when they arise. Also, because the Fire Service is a customer-focused service, the firefighter needs to be committed to delivering an excellent service. The role also includes training and maintaining competence through the Integrated Personal Development System.

Firefighters are also constantly looking for ways to reduce the risk of fire and providing advice to the public upon request. Maintaining an operational readiness is also key to the role, making sure that all equipment is serviced and ready for use. Having the ability to work as an effective team member is essential and having a good knowledge of Health and Safety is also important.

Sample generic interview question 3

What is Community Fire Safety?

If you are serious about becoming a firefighter then you should have a good knowledge of Community Fire Safety.

Before preparing your answer to this question, read the Community Fire Safety section of this guide in order to get a basic understanding of what it involves. I also recommend that you visit the website of the Fire Service you are applying to join, so that you can get a feel for what approach they are taking in relation to CFS. You may also wish to visit the Government's own Community Fire Safety site to get some more useful tips about this important subject.

Now take a look at the following sample response.

Generic interview question 3 – sample response

What is Community Fire Safety?

Community Fire Safety is one of the core elements of the firefighter's role.

It is about informing and educating the public with safety information that will help them to reduce the risk of fire in the home to nearly zero. It covers many different areas ranging from information relating to smoke alarms, Home Fire Safety Checks, electrical fire safety and cooking safety to name but a few.

I am aware that the Fire Service is constantly looking for ways to reduce fire deaths and injuries in the home through its effective Community Fire Safety reduction strategies.

Community Fire Safety is also about working with other agencies including the police and Social Services to establish ways of making the community safer together as opposed to working in isolation.

I visited your website and noticed that you have been working with Help the Aged to provide smoke alarms for the elderly, which is a good example of agencies working together to help save lives.

Sample generic interview question 4

If a member of the public asked you how to call the Fire Service, what advice would you give them?

This question is not a common one but there have been occasions when it has been asked during the firefighter interview. If you are going to be a firefighter then you certainly should know how to call the Fire Service in the event of an emergency.

The answer is a simple one and the following is a sample response to help you.

Generic interview question 4 – sample response

If a member of the public asked you how to call the Fire Service, what advice would you give them?

I would tell them to dial 999 using the nearest available working phone.

I'd also inform them that they can use their mobile phone to dial 999 even if they do not have any credit available.

I would tell them that they would be connected to a central call handling centre where they will be asked which service they require.

I would tell them that they must ask for the Fire Service. Once they are through to the Fire Service operator they will be asked a series of important questions. I would tell them to listen carefully to the Fire Service operator and answer all the questions carefully and accurately. It is important that they remain calm when making the call so that the operator can obtain all of the information.

I would tell them that the type of questions they will be asked are:

- *what the emergency is (e.g. fire, car crash, flood, person trapped, etc.)*

- *where it is (e.g. full address if known, name of road, prominent landmark)*

- *how many people are involved, if any*

- *any special problems/hazards that they need to know about.*

I would finally inform them that it is important only to use the 999 service when it is genuinely needed and that hoax calls should never be made.

Sample generic interview question 5

Do you have any experience of working as a team member?

The ability to work effectively in a team is an extremely important aspect of the firefighter's role. Not only will you be spending a great deal of time together at work, you will also depend on your colleagues during highly dangerous and stressful incidents. Therefore, it is important for you to demonstrate that you have the ability to work as an effective team member.

When responding to this type of question, think of occasions when you have been part of a team and achieved a common goal.

Maybe you are already involved in team sports playing hockey, rugby or football? You may also find that you have experience of working as a team member through work. If you have no or very little experience of working as a team member then try to get some before you apply to the Fire Service. After all, teamwork is an important aspect of the role.

Now take a look at the following sample response.

Generic interview question 5 – sample response

Do you have any experience of working as a team member?

Yes, I have many years' experience of working in a team environment.

To begin with, I have been playing hockey for my local team for the last three years. We worked really hard together improving our skills over the course of last season and we managed to win the league.

I am also very much involved in teamwork in my current job. I work as a nurse at the local hospital and in order for the ward to function correctly we must work effectively as a team. My job is to check all of the patients at the beginning of my shift and also make sure that we have enough medical supplies to last the duration. It is then my responsibility to inform the ward sister that the checks have been carried out. She will then obtain more supplies if we need them.

We have to work very closely together for many hours and we all pull together whenever the going gets tough. I enjoy working in a team environment and feel comfortable while working under pressure.

Sample generic interview question 6

Do you have any experience of working within the community?

Because the firefighter's role is very much community based, the Fire Service want to know that you are able to work with people from all backgrounds.

Many people would not feel comfortable working in the community, but as a firefighter it is an essential part of your role. Firefighters have very good reputations for being caring, helpful and considerate people who will help out wherever possible. While working as a firefighter you will be out in the community

promoting Fire Safety, visiting people's homes to offer fire safety advice and fitting smoke alarms, and so on. Therefore, it is important that you can provide examples of where you have already carried out some form of community work.

Community work can involve many different things ranging from Neighbourhood Watch to charity work or voluntary work.

Take a look at the following sample response.

Generic interview question 6 – sample response

Do you have any experience of working within the community?

I recently organised a charity boot fair at my local school. This was to raise money for a nearby hospital that wanted to buy some new medical equipment. I worked with a number of different people in the community to get the event off the ground.

I worked closely with the local school and advertised the boot fair in the local paper to generate some interest. I contacted local community groups such as Neighbourhood Watch to try to promote the event, which worked very well. The boot fair was attended by more than 500 people and we managed to raise over £750 for the good cause. I wouldn't have been able to arrange the event without working closely with different people and groups from within the community.

The event was a great success and I plan to organise another one next year.

Sample generic interview question 7

What do you understand by the term diversity?

You are almost guaranteed to be asked a question that relates to diversity and working with people from different cultures and backgrounds.

One of the Personal Qualities and Attributes of a firefighter is the ability to work with others. Over the last few years, senior Fire Service stakeholders, in collaboration with the Government, have taken up the challenge to work towards a more diverse workforce. Therefore, an understanding of what diversity means, and how important it is to the Fire Service, is crucial if you are to become a firefighter. This particular question is designed to see if you understand what the term diversity means in relation to the Fire Service.

Take a look at the following sample response to this question.

Generic interview question 7 – sample response

What do you understand by the term diversity?

The term diversity means different and varied things.

For example, if the Fire Service has a diverse workforce, it means that the people in that workforce are from different backgrounds, cultures and genders. The community in which we live is extremely diverse. Therefore, it is important that the Fire Service represents the community in which it serves so that a high level of service can be maintained. This gives the public more confidence in the Fire Service.

There are also other added benefits of a diverse workforce. It enables the Fire Service to reach every part of the community and provide Fire Safety advice to everybody as opposed to just certain individual groups of people.

Sample generic interview question 8

What do you understand about the term Health and Safety and who is responsible for it?

Health and Safety plays a very important part in the firefighter's working day.

As a firefighter you will be acutely aware of Health and Safety and how it affects you and your colleagues. Health and Safety is the responsibility of everybody at work. You are responsible for the safety of yourself and for the safety of everybody else. Health and Safety within the Fire Service is governed by the Health and Safety at Work Act 1974 and the Management of Health and Safety at Work Regulations 1999.

Make sure you are aware of the term 'risk assessment' and what it means to the operational firefighter.

The following is a sample response to this type of question.

Generic interview question 8 – sample response

What do you understand about the term Health and Safety and who is responsible for it?

Everybody is responsible for Health and Safety at work. Health and Safety is governed by the Health and Safety at Work Act 1974 and the Management of Health and Safety at Work Regulations 1999. Firefighters are responsible for the safety of themselves and the safety of each other.

Health and Safety is all about staying safe and promoting good working practices. In the Fire Service this means making sure that all protective clothing is usable and in good working order, checking that equipment and machinery is serviceable and carrying out risk assessments when required. It also includes simple things like making sure warning signs are put in place after the fire station bays have been cleaned.

It applies both when attending fires and incidents and also when carrying out duties around the station. Health and Safety should be at the forefront of everybody's mind when at work.

Sample generic interview question 9

What do you understand about the term Equality and Fairness?

Treating everybody with respect and dignity is important in everyday life. Treat others how you would expect to be treated regardless of their age, gender, sexual orientation or cultural background.

If you are not capable of treating people with respect and dignity then the Fire Service is not for you!

A question based on this subject is likely to come up during the interview and it relates to the PQA 'working with others'.

The following is a sample response to this question.

Generic interview question 9 – sample response

What do you understand about the term Equality and Fairness?

Equality and Fairness is about treating people with dignity and respect and without discrimination. Unfair discrimination in employment is wrong. It is bad for the individuals who are denied jobs or who suffer victimisation or harassment because of prejudice. I understand that within the Fire Service it is the responsibility of everyone to uphold the principles and policies of the organisation in relation to Equality and Fairness.

Discrimination or unacceptable behaviour of any sort is not tolerated and nor should it be. Not only is it important to apply these principles while working with colleagues in the Fire Service but it also applies when serving the public.

Sample generic interview question 10

If you witnessed a member of your team being bullied or harassed at work, what action would you take and why?

There is only one answer to this question and that is that you would take action to stop it, providing it was safe to do so. Bullying or harassment of any kind must not be tolerated. The second part of the question is just as important. They are asking you why you would take this particular action.

Before you prepare your answer to this question think carefully about what action you would take if somebody was being bullied or harassed. Taking action can mean a number of different things ranging from reporting the incident to your manager, through to intervention.

Whatever answer you give it is important that you are honest and tell the truth about how you would respond to such a situation. Take a look at the following sample response to this question.

Generic interview question 10 – sample response

If you witnessed a member of your team being bullied or harassed at work, what action would you take and why?

I would stop it immediately if it was safe to do so. This type of behaviour is totally unacceptable and must not be tolerated in the workplace.

The reason why I would take action is because if I didn't, then I would effectively be condoning the bullying or harassment. The type of action I would take would very much depend on the circumstances. In most cases I would intervene at the time of the incident and ask the person to stop the bullying or harassment.

If the incident were very serious, then I would report it to my manager so that further action could be taken. Whatever the situation was, I would definitely take steps to stop it from happening. I believe that I would also have a duty under Fire Service policy to take action to stop bullying and harassment.

Sample generic interview question II

What would be your reaction if someone you were working with was acting in an offensive manner? (Racially or sexually)

This kind of behaviour is not tolerated and therefore you should be asking the person to stop acting in this offensive manner.

This type of behaviour includes any form of racial or sexual jokes and again, these are not tolerated within the UK Fire Service. The Fire Service has strict policies in relation to this kind of unacceptable behaviour and it will not be tolerated.

When responding to questions of this nature, you should say that you would take steps to stop the person from acting in this manner, either through intervention or reporting. However, only ever say these words if you actually mean it. Do not lie.

Take a look at the following sample response.

Generic interview question 11 – sample response

What would be your reaction if someone you were working with was acting in an offensive manner? (Racially or sexually)

I would ask the person to stop. That would be my first action. This kind of behaviour is not acceptable. If I was to ignore it then I would be just as bad as the person who was carrying out the act.

I would then inform my line manager about the behaviour so that he/she could decide if any further action needed to be taken.

 how2become

Sample generic interview question 12

What qualities do you possess that would be of benefit to the Fire Service?

Questions based around 'qualities' are designed to assess that you have the right Personal Qualities and Attributes to become a firefighter. Therefore, your response should be predominantly based around these. However, it is still important to remember that a firefighter has many other qualities aside from these and you should try to include them too, where possible.

Take a look at the following sample response before constructing your own.

Generic interview question 12 – sample response

What qualities do you possess that would be of benefit to the Fire Service?

To begin with, I am a physically fit person who takes pride in my appearance. I am punctual, reliable and can be trusted to carry out a task on time and to a high standard.

I am a very good team worker and work well with other people. I can also be relied upon to work on my own, unsupervised, wherever necessary. I have good problem-solving skills, which have been obtained through my practical working background.

I am a confident person who is always looking to improve, learn and develop new skills. I am extremely adaptable and I am always open to new ideas. I view change as a positive thing and enjoy the challenges that this brings.

I have very good communication skills, both written and verbal, and I am committed to working hard for my employer, whoever that may be.

Sample generic interview question 13

Can you tell me a time when you have made a bad decision in your life and how you dealt with it?

Not a common question, but one that has been asked on a number of occasions. This is quite a difficult one to answer as we have all made bad decisions in our life and anybody who says that they haven't is probably not telling the truth.

However, the response that you give is important. You need to provide an example that doesn't put you across in a bad light.

The second part of the question is just as important. How you deal with situations or mistakes that you have made in your life is a good indication of your character and maturity.

Take a look at the example we have provided on the following page before preparing your own based on your individual experiences.

Generic interview question 13 – sample response

Can you tell me a time when you have made a bad decision in your life and how you dealt with it?

Yes. About five years ago I was working at a local shop stacking shelves and working behind the counter serving customers. I was working very hard for six days a week for a very low salary.

I was unhappy in the job because of the poor wages and although, I liked my boss, I felt that it was not worth working so hard for such poor wages, so I decided to leave.

I then found myself in a position having to find a new job without any money. I was studying at night school to gain an educational qualification and therefore needed some money

for books and study material. Leaving the job without having another one to go to was a bad decision on my part. I should have waited until I found another job before leaving.

However, I didn't get down about it. I immediately started looking for further employment and after two weeks I managed to get a job as a customer sales adviser for a local car retail firm, which I enjoyed very much.

If I make a bad decision in life I always try to take steps to rectify it, but more importantly learn from it. I believe it is important to evaluate and reflect on the important decisions we make in life.

Sample generic interview question 14

What would you do if you witnessed a friend in the Fire Service stealing?

There is only one answer to this question and that is to report the person who is stealing. Firefighters are trusted in the community and relied upon to be open, honest and reliable.

You will find that you will attend many incidents where you will be going in people's homes, vehicles or property and the Fire Service trusts you to act in accordance with their policies and procedures.

The following is a sample response to this question.

Generic interview question 14 – sample response

What would you do if you witnessed a friend in the Fire Service stealing?

I would report the incident to my line manager. Of course, it would be a difficult decision to make because that person is my friend and colleague. However, I would not like it if a firefighter was stealing from my house or property and

therefore it should be stopped immediately. I would also say that any person who steals from others is no friend of mine.

I would choose the appropriate time to inform my line manager about the incident. I understand that firefighters are trusted people in society and anything that does harm to that reputation should be challenged.

Sample generic interview question 15

What are the current Community Fire Safety activities of this Fire and Rescue Service?

A question that relates to Community Fire Safety is more than likely to come up during the interview. Remember to read the Community Fire Safety section of this guide to get a basic understanding of the type of advice the UK's firefighters are giving the public.

Make sure that you visit the website of the Fire and Rescue Service you are applying for. On this you will find some useful information that relates to CFS and what the Fire Service is doing to make the community a safer place.

Take a look at the following sample response to this question before constructing your own.

Generic interview question 15 – sample response

What are the current Community Fire Safety activities of this Fire and Rescue Service?

Having visited your website and spoken to serving firefighters at my local fire station, I understand that you are currently carrying out a number of Home Fire Safety Checks in people's homes to try to reduce the number of accidental house fires and injuries.

I also noticed that you are working closely with other agencies such as the police to reduce the number of deliberate vehicle fires that are occurring. I have also visited the Government's website to see what is happening on a national scale.

I particularly liked the 'checklist' that you provide on your website so that members of the public can make sure that they are doing all they can to keep themselves safe from fire.

Sample generic interview question 16

How do you keep yourself fit and why do you think fitness is important to the role of a firefighter?

Fitness is an important element of the firefighter's role.

As an operational firefighter you will have a duty to keep yourself physically fit and active. This question is quite simple to answer providing that you do actually carry out some form of physical exercise. If you do not then now is a good time to start. If you play a team sport then again this would be an advantage.

Eating properly is also key to maintaining a healthy lifestyle. While you are unlikely to be asked questions about your diet, you will find that you feel a whole lot better about yourself if you eat properly.

The following is a sample response to this question, based on a person who lives a healthy lifestyle and keeps physically fit.

Generic interview question 16 – sample response

How do you keep yourself fit and why do you think fitness is important to the role of a firefighter?

I keep myself fit and active and it is an important part of my life. I go swimming three times a week and swim 30 lengths every time I go.

I also go jogging twice a week to break up the routine and mix in some light weight work at the gym every now and again.

I play football for my local Sunday team, which involves one practice session every fortnight. Plus I ensure that I eat a proper diet, which helps to keep me feeling confident and healthy.

I think that fitness is vital to the role of a firefighter. The role involves working unsociable hours and I understand that it can be highly stressful at times. Coupled with the fact that the work can be physically demanding, it is important that firefighters stay fit and healthy so that they can perform to their peak and cope with the demands of the job.

Sample generic interview question 17

Have you ever had any experience of taking responsibility?

Firefighters must be responsible people.

You are responsible for your own safety and the safety of your work colleagues. You are responsible for looking after your personal protective equipment and for turning up for work on time and being prepared. A question based around responsibility is likely during the firefighter interview so we recommend that you take the time to think up an example of where you have had to take responsibility. This can either be in your working life, social or home life.

Take a look at the following sample response before creating your own response based on your own individual circumstances.

Generic interview question 17 – sample response

Have you ever had any experience of taking responsibility?

Yes, I am a single parent who has a great deal of responsibility every day of the week. I look after my two children, making sure they get to school every morning on time, before going to work myself.

My current day job is as a customer sales representative for a large retail outlet. Within this role I also have many responsibilities, which include the supervision of stocktaking and ensuring that all goods are ordered on time.

After I have finished work I pick up my children from the childcare centre before going home and helping them with their homework. I basically have responsibility for the total running of the house and making sure that everything runs smoothly.

I enjoy the challenge of responsibility and understand that it is an important aspect of the firefighter's role.

Sample generic interview question 18

What do you think are the important elements of communicating with different groups of people?

A question based around your communication skills is likely to appear during the firefighter interview. This question is designed to assess two parts of the Firefighter Personal Qualities and Attributes – working with others and effective communication skills.

Remember that firefighters have to be good communicators and be capable of working with people from every part of the community.

The following is a sample response to this question to help you structure your own.

Generic interview question 18 – sample response

What do you think are the important elements of communicating with different groups of people?

Effective communication skills are an integral part of the Firefighter Personal Qualities and Attributes. One of the main elements is respect. Being respectful of people's backgrounds and trying to appreciate how they feel about things, particularly the Fire Service, is important so that good relationships can be built.

Listening effectively is also another important aspect of good communication. Listening to what people say and getting feedback is important so that improvements can be made.

When communicating, it is vital that firefighters create an approachable and positive image so that trust can be built. Asking questions is important too so that you can understand what the different groups' needs are.

CHAPTER 13
FINAL INTERVIEW TIPS AND ADVICE

- If you have prepared yourself fully leading up to the interview you should have the confidence to perform to the best of your ability on the day. As I mentioned at the beginning of this book, preparation is key to your success so take the time to follow the instructions and guidance provided within this section.

- Make sure you know the correct date, time and location of your interview and be there early, with plenty of time to spare.

- Take into account the possibility of heavy traffic, a breakdown and parking problems, and so on.

- It is a good idea to make sure you know exactly where you are going. I recommend you visit the interview location prior to the day so you are familiar with the venue and how to get there.

- Ensure you have revisited your application form. The interview panel may ask you questions about its content so make sure you know what you submitted.

- Ensure you know both about the role of the firefighter and information relating to the actual Fire and Rescue Service you are applying to join.

- Have a good understanding about Community Fire Safety before attending the interview.

- Take a look at the Fire Service's website and find out what is current, such as Community Fire Safety campaigns, Integrated Risk Management, and so on.

- It is always a good idea to arrange a visit to a fire station before your interview. Ask the firefighters questions about their role and their working day so that you are fully prepared for your interview.

- Have knowledge of Health and Safety and in particular the five steps to risk assessment.

- Be aware of the Race Equality Scheme for the Fire Service you are applying to join. You could be asked a question about Equality and Fairness during your interview.

- Be aware of the Personal Qualities and Attributes that relate to the role of the firefighter. These are the areas that you will be assessed against. You must be able to provide specific examples of each key area.

- Make sure you dress smartly. Image is important in any interview and demonstrates that you are serious about the whole process. If you turn up in jeans and trainers the interviewer may view this as negative. If you want more interview advice then you can purchase the 'How to pass the Firefighter Interview' DVD through the website www. how2become.co.uk.

- Check whether you are required to take anything with you such as references, certificates, driving licence or proof of your educational qualifications.

- Remember to smile during the interview and be positive.

- Think of two possible questions to ask at the end of the interview. Try not to be clever when asking questions but instead ask questions that are relevant such as 'Where is the organisation planning to go with Community Fire Safety?'.

- When you enter the interview room make sure you are polite and say 'hello', 'good morning' or 'good afternoon'. Saying nothing at all will come across as being rude.

- Don't sit down until invited to do so. While this is not essential it does demonstrate good manners.

- Make sure you sit comfortably and don't slouch. A good posture will speak volumes about your confidence and determination to succeed.

- Think before you answer any questions. There is nothing wrong with pausing for a second to think about your answer. If you are unsure, ask the interviewer to repeat the question.

- Look interested when the panel ask you questions and be positive in your answers.

- If you are unsure of an answer try not to 'waffle' or make something up. If you can't answer a question just be honest and move on.

- Speak up when answering any questions and make positive eye contact. This doesn't mean staring out the interviewer!

- Finally, don't over-use your hands. Some hand movement or expression is good but too much can be distracting.

FREE BONUS GUIDE – HOW TO GET FIREFIGHTER FIT

Introduction

Welcome to your FREE 'How to Get Firefighter Fit' information guide. Within this guide you will find some very useful tips for helping you get, and stay, firefighter fit.

The firefighter fitness test is not difficult providing you put in the time and effort to reach a good all-round level of fitness. I recommend that you do not spend hours in the gym lifting heavy weights but rather aim for a varied and diverse fitness programme that cover exercises such as swimming, rowing, jogging, brisk walking and light weight work.

In addition to getting fit, keep an eye on your diet and eat healthy foods while drinking plenty of water. It will all go a long way to helping you improve your general well-being and concentration levels.

Planning your workouts and preparing for the firefighter physical tests

Most people who embark on a fitness regime in January have given it up by February. The reason why most people give up their fitness regime so soon is mainly owing to a lack of proper preparation. You will recall that throughout this guide the word 'preparation' has been integral, and the same word applies when preparing for the physical tests. Preparation is key to your success and it is essential that you plan your workouts effectively.

Firefighters are inherently physically fit people. Some of them will be keen runners while others will be keen weight trainers. In the build-up to the physical tests I advise you to concentrate on specific exercises that will allow you to pass the tests with ease. These exercises may not be what you expect, simply because they are not based around lifting heavy weights or running marathon distances!

Read on for some great ways to pass the firefighter physical tests and stay firefighter fit all year round.

Get an assessment before you start training

The first step is to get a fitness test at the gym, weigh yourself and run your fastest mile. Once you have done all three of these you should write down your results and keep them hidden away somewhere safe. After a month of following your new fitness regime, do all three tests again and check your results against the previous month's. This is a great way to monitor your performance and progress and it will also keep you motivated and focused on your goals.

Keep a check on what you eat and drink

Make sure you write down everything you eat and drink for a whole week. You must include tea, water, milk, biscuits, and

anything and everything that you digest. You will soon begin to realise how much you are eating and you will notice areas in which you can make some changes. For example, if you are taking sugar with your tea then why not try reducing it or giving it up all together. If you do then you will soon notice the difference.

It is important that you start to look for opportunities to improve your fitness and well-being right from the offset. These areas are what I call 'easy wins'.

You don't need to go to a gym in order to prepare for the firefighter physical tests

When I applied to join the Fire Service the physical tests were rigorous, demanding and extremely difficult to pass. As part of the assessment I was required to bench press 50 kg, 20 times within 60 seconds! Thankfully those tests no longer form part of the selection process. It is my strong belief that you do not have to attend a gym in order to pass the tests. However, to cater for the gym people out there I have included a number of exercises within this guide which specifically require you to attend a gym.

Walking is one of the best exercises you can do as part of your preparation for the firefighter physical tests. While it shouldn't be the only form of exercise you carry out, it will go a long way to improving your focus and general well-being. Now, when I say 'walking' I don't mean a gentle stroll, I mean 'brisk' walking. Try walking at a fast pace for 30 minutes every day for a seven-day period. Then see how you feel at the end of the seven-day period. I guarantee you'll begin to feel a lot healthier and fitter. Brisk walking is also a fantastic way to lose weight if you think you need to.

There are some more great exercises contained within this guide and most of them can be carried out without the need to attend a gym.

One step at a time

Only you will know how fit you are. I advise that, first of all, you write down the areas that you believe or feel you need to improve on. For example, if you feel that you need to work on your upper body strength then pick out exercises from this guide that will work on that area for you.

The key to making improvements is to do it gradually, and at one step at a time. Try to set yourself small goals. If you think you need to lose 2 stone (13 kg) in weight then focus on losing a few pounds at a time. For example, during the first month aim to lose 6 pounds (3 kg) only. Once you have achieved this then again aim to lose another 6 pounds over the next month, and so on and so forth. The more realistic your goal, the more likely you are to achieve it. One of the biggest problems that people encounter when starting a fitness regime is they become bored quickly. This then leads to a lack of motivation and desire, and soon the fitness programme stops.

Change your exercise routine often. Instead of walking try jogging. Instead of jogging try cycling with the odd day of swimming. Keep your workouts varied and interesting to ensure that you stay focused and motivated.

Stretching

How many people stretch before carrying out any form of exercise? Very few people is the correct answer. Not only is it irresponsible but it is also placing yourself at high risk from injury. Before we commence with the exercises we will take a look at a few warm-up stretches. Make sure you stretch fully before carrying out any exercises. You want your Fire Service career to be a long one and that means looking after yourself, including stretching! It is also very important to check with your GP that you are medically fit to carry out any form of physical exercise.

The warm-up calf stretch

To perform this stretch effectively you should first start by facing a wall while standing upright. Your right foot should be close to the wall and your right knee bent. Now place your hands flat against the wall and at a height that is level with your shoulders. Stretch your left leg far out behind you without lifting your toes and heel off the floor, and lean towards the wall.

Once you have performed this stretch for 25 seconds, switch legs and carry out the same procedure for the left leg. As with all exercises contained within this guide, stop if you feel any pain or discomfort.

Stretching the shoulder muscles

To begin with, stand with your feet slightly apart and with your knees only slightly bent. Now hold your arms right out in front of you and with your palms facing away from you with your fingers pointing skywards. Now place your right palm on the back of your left hand and use it to push the left hand further away from you. If you are performing this exercise correctly then you will feel the muscles in your shoulder stretching. Hold for 10 seconds before switching sides.

Stretching the quad muscles (front of the thigh)

Before you carry out any form of brisk walking or running then it is imperative that you stretch your leg muscles. During the firefighter physical tests the instructors should take you through a series of warm-up exercises which will include stretching the quad muscles.

To begin with, stand with your right hand pressed against the back of a wall or firm surface. Bend your left knee and bring your left heel up to your bottom while grasping your foot with your left hand. Your back should be straight and your shoulders, hips and knees should all be in line at all times

during the exercise. Hold for 25 seconds before switching legs.

Stretching the hamstring muscles (back of the thigh)

It is very easy to injure your hamstring muscles as a firefighter. Imagine all of the running and climbing up and down ladders that you'll do during your career. Therefore, you must get into the routine of stretching out the hamstring muscles before every drill or training session.

To perform this exercise correctly, stand up straight and place your right foot onto a table or other firm surface so that your leg is almost parallel to the floor. Keep your left leg straight and your foot at a right angle to your leg. Slowly start to move your hands down your right leg towards your ankle until you feel tension on the underside of your thigh. When you feel this tension you know that you are starting to stretch the hamstring muscles. Hold for 25 seconds before switching legs.

We have covered only a small number of stretching exercises here; however, it is crucial that you stretch out fully in all areas before carrying out any of the following exercises. Remember to obtain professional advice before carrying out any type of exercise.

Running

One of the great ways to prepare for the firefighter physical tests is to embark on a structured running programme. You do not need to run at a fast pace, or even run for long distances, in order to gain massively from this type of exercise.

Before I joined the Fire Service I spent a few years in the Royal Navy. I applied to join the Navy when I was 16 and I made it through the selection process with ease until I reached the medical. During the medical the doctor told me that I was overweight and that I had to lose a stone before

Tips for Running

- As with any exercise you should consult a doctor before taking part to make sure that you are medically fit.

- It is certainly worth investing in a pair of comfortable running shoes that serve the purpose for your intended training programme. Your local sports shop will be able to advise you on the types that are best for you. You don't have to spend a fortune to buy a good pair of running shoes.

- It is a good idea to invest in a 'high visibility' jacket or coat so that you can be seen by fast-moving traffic if you intend to run on or near the road.

- Make sure you carry out at least five whole minutes of stretching exercises not only before but also after your running programme. This can help to prevent injury.

- While you shouldn't run on a full stomach, it is also not good to run on an empty one either. A great food to eat approximately 30 minutes before a run is a banana. This is excellent for giving you energy.

- Drink plenty of water throughout the day. Try to drink at least 1.5 litres each day in total. This will keep you hydrated and help to prevent muscle cramp.

- Don't overdo it. If you feel any pain or discomfort then stop and seek medical advice.

they would accept me. To be honest, I was heart-broken. I couldn't believe it, especially after all that hard work I had put in preparing for the tests and the interview! Anyway, as soon as I arrived back home from the medical I started out on a structured running programme that would see me lose the stone in weight within only four weeks! The following running programme is very similar to one I used all those years ago and it will serve you well when preparing for the firefighter physical tests.

Before I provide you with the running programme, however, make sure you have read the important running tips in the box on the previous page.

Running programme week 1

DAY 1

- Run a total of 3 miles only at a steady pace.

If you cannot manage 3 miles then try the following:

- Walk at a brisk pace for half a mile or approximately 10 minutes.

Then

- Run for 1 mile or 8 minutes.

Then

- Walk for another half a mile or approximately 10 minutes.

Then

- Run for 1.5 miles or 12 minutes.

Walking at a brisk pace is probably the most effective way to lose weight if you need to. It is possible to burn the same amount of calories if you walk the same distance as if you were running.

When walking at a 'brisk' pace it is recommended that you walk as fast as is comfortably possible without breaking into a run or slow jog.

DAY 2

- Walk for 2 miles or approximately 20 minutes at a brisk pace.

Then

- Run for 2 miles or 14 minutes.

DAY 3

- Repeat day one.

DAY 4

- Walk at a brisk pace for 0.5 miles or approximately 7 minutes.

Then

- Run for 3 miles or 20 minutes.

DAY 5

- Repeat day one.

DAY 6 AND DAY 7

- Rest days. No exercise.

Running programme week 2

DAY 1

- Run for 4 miles or 25 minutes.

DAY 2

- Run a total of 3 miles at a steady pace.

If you cannot manage 3 miles then try the following:

- Walk at a brisk pace for half a mile or approximately 10 minutes.

Then

- Run for 1 mile or 8 minutes.

Then

- Walk for another half a mile or approximately 10 minutes.

Then

- Run for 1.5 miles or 12 minutes.

DAY 3

- Rest day. No exercise.

DAY 4

- Run for 5 miles or 35–40 minutes.

DAY 5

- Run for 3 miles or 20 minutes.

Then

- Walk at a brisk pace for 2 miles or approximately 20 minutes.

DAY 6

- Run for 5 miles or 35–45 minutes.

DAY 7

- Rest day. No exercise.

Once you have completed the second week running programme, use the third week to perform different types of exercises, such as cycling and swimming. During week 4 you can then commence the two-week running programme again. You'll be amazed at how much easier it is the second time around!

When preparing for the firefighter selection process, use your exercise time as a break from your studies. For example, if you have been practising numerical reasoning tests for an hour, why not take a break and go running? When you return from your run you can then concentrate on your studies feeling refreshed.

Now that I've provided you with a structured running programme to follow, there really are no excuses. So, get out there and start running! I'll now provide you with a number of key targeted exercises that will allow you to prepare effectively for the firefighter physical tests.

Exercises that will improve your ability to pass the firefighter physical tests

Press-ups

While running is a great way to improve your overall fitness, you will also need to carry out exercises that improve your upper body strength. These exercises will help you to pass the firefighter physical tests where you need to carry heavy items of equipment or drag a casualty over a prolonged distance.

The great thing about press-ups is that you don't have to attend a gym to perform them. However, you must ensure that you can do them correctly as injury can occur. You only need to spend five minutes every day on press-ups, possibly after you go running or even before if you prefer. If you are not used to doing press-ups then start slowly and aim to carry out at least ten.

Even if you struggle to do just ten, you will soon find that after a few days' practice at these you will be up to 20 or more.

Step 1 – To begin with, lie on a mat or even surface. Your hands should be shoulder-width apart and your arms fully extended.

Step 2 – Gradually lower your body until the elbows reach 90°. Do not rush the movement as you may cause injury.

Step 3 – Once your elbows reach 90° slowly return to the starting position with your arms fully extended.

The press-up action should be a continuous movement with no rest. However, it is important that the exercise is as smooth as possible and there should be no jolting or sudden movements. Try to complete as many press-ups as possible and always keep a record of how many you do. This will keep your focus and also maintain your motivation levels.

Did you know that the world record for non-stop press-ups is currently 10,507 set in 1980?

WARNING – Ensure you take advice from a competent fitness trainer in relation to the correct execution of press-up exercises and other exercises contained within this guide.

Sit-ups

Sit-ups are great for building the core stomach muscles. Strong abdominal muscles are important for lifting items of a equipment, something which is integral to the role of a firefighter.

At the commencement of the exercise lie flat on your back with your knees bent at a 45° angle and with your feet together. Your hands can either be crossed on your chest, by your sides, or cupped behind your ears as indicated in the diagram opposite.

Without moving your lower body, curl your upper torso upwards and in towards your knees, until your shoulder blades are as high off the ground as possible. As you reach the highest point, tighten your abdominal muscles for a second. This will allow you to get the most out of the exercise. Now slowly start

to lower yourself back to the starting position. You should be aiming to work up to at least 50 effective sit-ups every day. You will be amazed at how quickly this can be achieved and you will begin to notice your stomach muscles developing.

While sit-ups do not form part of firefighter physical tests, they are still a great way of improving your all-round fitness and therefore should not be neglected.

Pull-ups

Pull-ups are another great way for building the core upper body muscle groups which firefighters use while climbing ladders, lifting heavy items of equipment and even while wearing breathing apparatus. The unfortunate thing about this type of exercise is you will probably need to attend a gym in order to carry them out. Having said that, there are a number of different types of 'pull-up bars' available to buy on the market that can be fitted easily and safely to a doorway at home. If you choose to purchase one of these items make sure that it conforms to the relevant safety standards first.

Lateral pull-ups are very effective at increasing upper body strength. If you have access to a gymnasium then these can be practised on a 'lateral pull-down' machine. It is advised that you consult a gym member of staff about how to do these exercises.

Pull-ups should be performed by grasping firmly a sturdy and solid bar. Before you grasp the bar make sure it is safe. Your hands should be roughly shoulder-width apart. Straighten your arms so that your body hangs loose. You will feel your lateral muscles and biceps stretching as you hang in the air. This is the starting position for the lateral pull-up exercise.

Next, pull yourself upwards to the point where your chest is almost touching the bar and your chin is actually over the bar. While pulling upwards, focus on keeping your body straight without any arching or swinging as this can result in injury. Once your chin is over the bar, you can lower yourself back down to the initial starting position. Repeat the exercise ten times.

Squats (these work the legs and bottom)

Squats are a great exercise for working the leg muscles. They are the perfect exercise in your preparation for the firefighter physical tests as they relate to many of the tasks a firefighter is required to perform. Firefighters need to squat before carrying out any form of safe lifting technique and they also need to squat when working at ground level during operational incidents.

At the commencement of the exercise, stand up straight with your arms at your sides. Concentrate on keeping your feet shoulder-width apart and your head up. Do not look downwards at any point during the exercise. You will see from the diagram above that the person has their lower back slightly arched. They are also holding light weights which can add to the intensity of the exercise.

Now start to bend your knees very slowly while pushing your rear out as though you are about to sit down on a chair. Keep lowering yourself down until your thighs reach past the 90° point. Make sure your weight is on your heels so that your knees do not extend over your toes. At this point you may wish to tighten your thighs and buttocks to intensify the exercise.

As you come back up to a standing position, push down through your heels which will allow you to maintain your balance. Repeat the exercise 15 to 20 times.

Lunges (these work the thighs and bottom)

You will have noticed throughout this section of the guide that I have been providing you with simple, yet highly effective exercises that can be carried out at home. The lunge exercise is another great addition to the range of exercises that require no attendance at the gym. Lunges also fit perfectly into the role of a firefighter, simply because they concentrate on building the necessary core muscles to perform the demanding tasks of the job.

To begin with, stand with your back straight and your feet together (you may hold light hand weights if you wish to add some intensity to the exercise).

Next, take a big step forwards as illustrated in the diagram opposite, making sure you inhale as you go and landing with the heel first. Bend the front knee no more than 90° so as to avoid injury. Keep your back straight and lower the back knee as close to the floor as possible. Your front knee should be lined up over your ankle and your back thigh should be in line with your back.

To complete the exercise, exhale and push down against your front heel, squeezing your buttocks tight as you rise back to a starting position.

Try to repeat the exercise 15 to 20 times before switching sides.

Lateral raises (these work the shoulder muscles)

Think of the occasions as a firefighter when you would be required to use your shoulder muscles. The answer is during virtually every practical task that you carry out. From climbing ladders to lifting equipment and from wearing breathing apparatus to running out hose lengths you will use your shoulder muscles. Therefore, it is important that you carry out some form of shoulder muscle related exercises in your

preparation for the physical tests. My advice is that you perform lateral raises as part of your training programme as they are a fantastic exercise for building and developing the shoulder muscle groups.

Take a dumbbell in each hand and hold them by the sides of your body with the palms facing inward.

Stand or sit with your feet shoulder-width apart, knees slightly bent. Do not lean backwards as you could cause injury to your back. Raise your arms up and out to the sides until they are parallel to the ground, then lower them back down carefully. Repeat the exercise 15 to 20 times.

The above exercises will allow you to improve on your upper and lower body strength which will in turn improve your ability to pass the firefighter physical tests.

Alternative exercises

Swimming

Apart from press-ups, lateral raises and the other exercises I have provided, another fantastic way to improve your upper body and overall fitness is to go swimming. If you have access to a swimming pool, and you can swim, then this is a brilliant way to improve your fitness.

If you are not a great swimmer you can start off with short distances and gradually build up your swimming strength and stamina. Breaststroke is sufficient for building good upper body strength providing you put the effort into swimming an effective number of lengths. You may wish to alternate your running programme with the odd day of swimming. If you can swim 10 lengths of a 25 m pool initially then this is a good base to start from. You will soon find that you can increase this number easily providing that you carry on swimming every week. Try running to your local swimming pool if it is not too far away, swimming 20 lengths of breaststroke, and then running back home.

This is a great way to combine your fitness activity and prevent yourself from becoming bored with your training programme.

The multi-stage fitness test or bleep test

A great way to build endurance and stamina is by training with the multi-stage fitness test, or bleep test as it is otherwise called.

The multi-stage fitness test is used by sports coaches and trainers to estimate an athlete's VO2 Max (maximum oxygen uptake). The test is especially useful for players of sports like football, hockey or rugby. Some fire services still use this method of testing for their potential recruits and, therefore, you may find you will have to take this test during the selection process.

The test itself can be obtained through various websites on the internet and it is great for building your endurance and stamina levels.

Tips for staying with your workout

The hardest part of your training programme will be sticking with it. In this final part of your fitness guide I will provide some useful golden rules that will enable you to maintain your motivational levels in the build-up to the firefighter physical tests. In order to stay with your workout for longer, try following these simple rules:

Golden rule number one – Work out often

Aim to train three to five times each and every week.

Each training session should last between 20 minutes to a maximum of an hour. The quality of training is important so don't go for heavy weights but instead go for a lighter weight with a better technique. On days when you are feeling energetic, take advantage of this opportunity and do more!

Within this guide I have deliberately provided you with a number of 'simple to perform' exercises that are targeted at the core muscle groups required to perform the role of a firefighter. In between your study sessions try carrying out these exercises at home or get yourself out road running or cycling. Use your study 'down time' effectively and wisely.

Golden rule number two – Mix up your exercises

Your exercise programme should include some elements of cardiovascular (aerobics, running, brisk walking and cycling), resistance training (weights or own body exercises such as press-ups and sit-ups) and, finally, flexibility (stretching). Make sure that you always warm up and warm down.

If you are a member of a gym then consider taking up a class such as Pilates. This form of exercise class will teach you how to build core training into your exercise principles, and show you how to hit your abdominals in ways that are not possible with conventional sit-ups. If you are a member of a gym then a fantastic 'all round' exercise that I strongly recommend is rowing. Rowing will hit every major muscle group in your body and it is also perfect for improving your stamina levels and cardiovascular fitness.

Golden rule number three – Eat a healthy and balanced diet

It is vitally important that you eat the right fuel to give you the energy to train to your full potential. Don't fill your body with rubbish and then expect to train well. Think about what you are eating and drinking, including the quantities, and keep a record of what you are digesting. You will become stronger and fitter more quickly if you eat little amounts of nutritious foods at short intervals.

Golden rule number four – Get help

Try working with a personal trainer. They will ensure that you work hard and will help you to achieve your goals. If you cannot afford a personal trainer then try training with someone else. The mere fact that they are there at your side will add an element of competition to your training sessions!

A consultation with a professional nutritionist will also help you improve your eating habits and establish your individual food needs.

Golden rule number five – Fitness is for life

Working out and eating correctly are not short-term projects. They are things that should be as natural to us as brushing our teeth.

Make fitness a permanent part of your life by following these tips, and you'll lead a better and more fulfilling life!

Good luck and work hard to improve your weak areas.

A FEW FINAL WORDS

You have now reached the end of the guide and no doubt you will be ready to start preparing for the firefighter selection process. Just before you go off and start on your preparation, consider the following.

Throughout my life I have found a number of common attributes in those people who achieve success. These are as follows:

They believe in themselves

Regardless of what anyone tells you, you *can* become a firefighter. Just like any job of this nature, you have to be prepared to work hard in order to be successful. Make sure you have the self-belief to pass the selection process and fill your mind with positive thoughts.

They prepare fully

When I joined the Fire Service I was amazed at how many people said to me 'you're lucky to get a job in the Fire Service'. I didn't bother responding to comments like this because I knew 100 per cent that there was no luck involved in my success. It was down solely to the amount of preparation I had put in during the weeks and months leading up to the selection process. Those people who achieve in life prepare fully for every eventuality and that is what you must do when you apply to become a firefighter. Work very hard and especially concentrate on your weak areas.

They persevere

Perseverance is my favourite word. Everybody comes across obstacles or setbacks in their life, but it is what you do about those setbacks that is important. If I fail at something, then I want to know 'why' I've failed. This allows me to improve for next time and I always know that if I keep improving and trying, success will follow. Utilise this same method of thinking when you apply to become a firefighter.

They are self-motivated

How much do you want this job? Do you want it, or do you *really* want it?

When I applied to join the Fire Service I wanted it more than anything in the world. That self-motivation shone through on my application and during my interview. For the weeks and months leading up to firefighter selection, be motivated as best you can and always keep your fitness levels up as this will serve to increase your levels of motivation.

Work hard, stay focused and be what you want . . .

Richard McMunn

INDEX

Visit www.how2become.co.uk to find more related products that will help you to pass this selection process. From the website we can provide you with DVDs and guides that will help you to pass the interview, and other stages of the selection process. We also run one-day intensive training courses that are designed to help you successfully pass the application process for any career.

Visit www.how2become.co.uk for more details.